TERRORISM AND POLITICS

Also by Barry Rubin

ISLAMIC FUNDAMENTALISM IN EGYPTIAN POLITICS*
THE POLITICS OF TERRORISM: TERRORISM AS A STATE AND
    REVOLUTIONARY STRATEGY *(editor)*
THE POLITICS OF COUNTERTERRORISM: THE ORDEAL OF
    DEMOCRATIC STATES *(editor)*

*also published by St. Martin's Press

Terrorism and Politics

Edited by
Barry Rubin

St. Martin's Press
New York

in association with the Johns Hopkins
Foreign Policy Institute

First published in the United States of America in 1991

Printed in the United States of America

ISBN 0-312-06068-8

Library of Congress Cataloging-in-Publication Data
Terrorism and politics / edited by Barry Rubin.
     p. cm.
   Includes index.
   ISBN 0-312-06068-8
   1. Terrorism—Political aspects. 2. Terrorism—Prevention.
I. Rubin, Barry M.
HV6431.T4618 1991
363.3'2—dc20   91-8116
                CIP

Contents

Notes on the Contributors

William M. Carley, who holds a B.S. in journalism from Marquette University and an M.A. in political science from Stanford University, has been a *Wall Street Journal* reporter for 30 years. He has covered aviation for nearly 15 years and has written numerous articles on terrorism directed at airlines.

William V. Cowan retired from the U.S. Marine Corps in 1985. A graduate of the U.S. Naval Academy, he spent more than ten years on special assignments within the intelligence and special operations communities. From 1985 to 1987, he served on the staff of United States Senator Warren B. Rudman, helping coauthor the 1986 Special Operations legislation and serving as Senator Rudman's staff assistant to the Iran-contra hearings. Mr. Cowan has been involved in terrorism issues since 1983.

Nur Bilge Criss is assistant professor of international relations at Bilkent University in Ankara, Turkey. Previously, she served as associate director of alumni relations and development at George Washington University. She holds a PhD from George Washington University, an MA from the University of Florida, and a BA from the University of Ankara.

Michael Eisenstadt is a fellow at the Washington Institute for Near East Policy. He holds a B.A. from the State University of New York at Binghamton and an M.A. in Arab Studies from the Center for Contemporary Arab Studies at Georgetown University. Eisenstadt writes on Arab-Israeli military affairs and is author of *Sword of the Arabs: Iraq's Strategic Weapons*.

Allan Gerson is an attorney and author with substantial experience in international organizations. He served from 1981 to 1985 as chief counsel to the U.S. delegation to the United Nations and as a senior adviser to Ambassadors Jeane Kirkpatrick and Vernon Walters. In 1987, Mr. Gerson joined the American Enterprise Institute. He is the author of two books: *Lawyers' Ethics: Contemporary Dilemmas* and *Israel, the West Bank, and International Law.*

Joseph W. Marx is a Phi Beta Kappa graduate of the University of Notre Dame and a 1990 graduate of The Paul H. Nitze School of Advanced International Studies of Johns Hopkins University. At SAIS, Marx was a John M. Olin fellow in American foreign policy and security studies. Mr. Marx now serves as research assistant to President Richard Nixon.

Barry Rubin directs the Program for the Political Study of Terrorism at the Johns Hopkins Foreign Policy Institute and is a senior fellow of the Washington Institute for Near East Policy. Dr. Rubin is the author of 10 books, including *Instanbul Intrigues* and *Modern Dictators: Third World Coupmakers, Strongmen, and Populist Tyrants.*

Foreword

Barry Rubin

This book, the third and final volume of the Johns Hopkins Foreign Policy Institute's Project for the Political Study of Terrorism, deals with rarely studied, but extremely urgent, problems of terrorism and provides new material on these key issues.

Particularly new and fascinating is William V. Cowan's "Intelligence, Rescue, Retaliation, and Decision Making." Cowan is a retired colonel involved in undercover counterterrorism work and the preparation for efforts to rescue American hostages in Beirut. For the first time, he discusses details of these efforts. His main theme is to analyze two major problems in the U.S. response to terrorism: how the military's bureaucracy has blocked attempts to improve the functioning and coordination of special efforts and how politicians' reluctance to risk striking at terrorists has prevented the launching of rescue missions. His narrative and conclusions are indispensable to understanding the shortcomings of U.S. counterterrorism efforts despite the high attention and resources they have received.

Israel is a country particularly identified with success in counterterrorist operations. For the first time in English, Michael Eisenstadt, in "Special Operations Against Terrorism: The Israeli Approach," provides a detailed look at Israeli units, techniques, and decision making in this area. Two particular themes may apply to U.S. requirements, despite a number of important structural and strategic differences between the two countries.

First, rather than being marginalized, there are highly specialized counterterrorist units that enjoy the respect and support of the military high command. Second, there are clear and simple chains of command for operations, which reduce interservice rivalry and internal conflicts.

Eisenstadt's own experience as a U.S. Army officer and military analyst increase the value of his analysis and evaluation.

Allan Gerson brings to bear his extensive experience in the diplomatic struggle against terrorism. Gerson, a lawyer who served as a high-level official in the Departments of State and Justice, describes the battle in the 1970s and 1980s in which states sponsoring terrorism tried to justify such groups and acts as appropriate national liberation efforts. In "Legitimizing International Terrorism: Is the Campaign Over?" he suggests that this campaign has been defeated by a firm U.S. stand, rather than by appeasement. As Cowan also shows, the conflict between geopolitics and counterterrorism policy is unending, forcing leaders to make a number of difficult decisions on priorities.

The most spectacular and bloody terrorist actions of recent years have involved the planting of bombs on aircraft. Two chapters consider the efforts of terrorists and the countermeasures of airlines and governments. William M. Carley, a veteran *Wall Street Journal* reporter specializing in aviation, writes in "Airline Safety: The Price of Security" about the difficult trade-offs among cost, convenience, and counterterrorism. The huge volume of flights and luggage, the numbers of passengers, and narrow margins of times involved make the task of protecting these planes to be far more difficult than is generally realized. At the same time, however, the lack of clear responsibility between companies and governments—and the carelessness and minimal resources often given this matter—produce tragedies that might have been prevented. Carley provides a number of detailed case studies to illustrate these problems.

In "U.S. Strategy toward Aviation Security: A New Look," Joseph W. Marx, a former congressional staff member takes up some specific issues in the U.S. evaluation of how best to safeguard passenger planes. In particular, he looks at technical innovations that are more effective at uncovering explosives in luggage—but that are also expensive, sometimes difficult to operate, and raise problematic issues of their own. Marx also notes the kinds of difficulties the U.S. government has in trying to cajole and pressure other countries to improve security at their airports, where security breaches have usually occurred. Finally, he points to the controversial, often passionate, debate as to how, when, and whether governments and airlines should communicate intelligence warnings about threats against aviation.

The use of terrorism by certain political movements is often taken for granted. The two final chapters consider the rational political and strategic choices behind a strategy of terrorism. In "Mercenaries of Ideology: Turkey's Terrorism War," Professor Bilge Criss draws on a wide range of Turkish sources to provide the first history in English on the deployment of terrorism by extreme leftist and rightist groups in Turkey and the government's eventual suppression of them. In terms of purely terrorist methods, Turkey witnessed the most intensive and bloody such conflict in modern history. Dr. Criss shows how government shortcomings, including internal deadlock and efforts to use terrorist groups in party rivalries, greatly contributed to this crisis.

The Palestine Liberation Organization, perhaps more than any other current group, is associated with the use of terrorism over a long period. Barry Rubin, in "The Origins of PLO Terrorism," suggests that this was a carefully chosen strategy based on the organization's limitations—an inability to wage guerrilla war and historic disinterest in mass organizing—and on its evaluation of the enemy. Because the group wanted to destroy Israel and had no interest in compromise or negotiations, it was indifferent to the way terrorism polarized the situation and hurt its reputation. Terrorism mobilized Palestinian and Arab support for the PLO; PLO leaders expected that a sustained campaign would provoke Israel's collapse. But terrorism also had long-term effects within the PLO, creating ideological attitudes, extremist leaders, and internal violence, which paralyzed its ability to alter course.

These studies on terrorism are intended to be of both policy and scholarly interest. Aside from their own content, they will hopefully illustrate the usefulness of serious research in comprehending and combating terrorism.

TERRORISM AND POLITICS

1
Intelligence, Rescue, Retaliation, and Decision Making

William V. Cowan

I t is possible that few things are as frustrating to many Americans as our nation's obvious inability to deal effectively with either terrorism or terrorists. The direct impact, either real or potential, of terrorist acts on average Americans, highlighted by intense media coverage of major incidents during the past 10 or so years, has intensified U.S. awareness of terrorism.

As a nation, we agonized during the Tehran hostage crisis, only to have agony turn to despair when the military rescue effort crumbled in the Iranian desert.

The bombing of the U.S. embassy in Beirut in 1983, followed a few months later by the bombing of the U.S. Marine Compound and the killing of 241 U.S. Marines, demonstrated that even in an environment in which the threat was known to be significant, the United States was unable to collect adequate intelligence or defend diplomatic or military interests properly.

The summer 1985 incidents involving Trans World Airlines (TWA) Flight 847 and the *Achille Lauro*, together with the 1988 bombing of TWA Flight 103, highlighted the vulnerability of U.S. citizens abroad to terrorists. And the ongoing hostage crisis in Lebanon, highlighted by the death in 1989 of Marine Lieutenant Colonel Rich Higgins, provides testimony to the inability of the United States to deal with terrorism. To some of us who have worked closely with the counterterrorism issue, the question of U.S. impotence in dealing with terrorists deals more with a lack of leadership than with a lack of capabilities.

In December 1983, I was a member of a small, select team of military intelligence and special operations experts ordered to Beirut in the wake of the bombing of the U.S. Marine Compound. We were deployed at the specific direction of the chairman of the Joint Chiefs of Staff (JCS), and among our missions was one that called for providing recommendations on the way the United States might retaliate against those who had planned for and executed the bombing.

On the day the Marines were bombed, a French military compound in Beirut was also bombed. Fifty-six French soldiers were killed, and the next day French aircraft struck at known terrorist bases in Lebanon. Three days later, when terrorists used a similar truck bomb to attack an Israeli barracks in southern Lebanon, the Israelis, too, quickly responded with air strikes against known terrorist locations.

Meanwhile, here in the United States, the U.S. team awaited permission to proceed, while ranking military and civilian leaders in the Pentagon debated whether the team should go. Then, following their approval, the bureaucracy worked through an agonizingly slow coordination and approval process that involved the U.S. Army, the State Department, the Central Intelligence Agency (CIA), the Defense Intelligence Agency (DIA), and the U.S. European Command Headquarters in Stuttgart, Germany. We finally left for Beirut in early December 1983, some six weeks after the Marines had been bombed.

Once in Beirut, our team settled in quickly and began work. Two of us were very familiar with Beirut, and, within hours, we were out among the population collecting information needed to respond to our mission requirements. Some of our work was extremely dangerous; some was not. Throughout, however, we coordinated on a continuous basis with William Buckley, the CIA's station chief in Beirut. As part of our assigned mission, we developed a comprehensive list of military retaliatory options that our Beirut experience indicated were possible. Some involved highly sensitive intelligence operations that would penetrate the terrorists' sanctuaries. Others involved the precise use of military force against select targets. None, however, included specific recommendations that would have caused casualties among innocent civilians.

We spent nearly six weeks in Lebanon working on our assignments, and, prior to leaving, we gave Buckley a detailed briefing on our total mission, including our recommendations for retaliation against the terrorists who had bombed the Marines. Buckley voiced strong support, as did the deputy commander in chief of U.S. European Command when we briefed him in Stuttgart, Germany on our way back to the United States.

Once back in the United States, we submitted our report through the reporting chain of command to the chairman of the JCS. However, it quickly became mired in the bureaucracy of the Pentagon. No one, including those we worked for directly or those who had tasked us, championed our cause or worked to ensure that the report made its way quickly to the chairman. Some senior officers even expressed open hostility at the idea of retaliation, challenging us to defend our recommendations.

As weeks went by and our frustration mounted, a friend asked us to brief his immediate superior in the White House. His boss, Edward Hickey, was the director of the White House Military Office, and although he had direct access to the president, he was outside the national security structure.

We spent nearly an hour with Hickey, discussing each of our recommendations and responding to his questions. At the end of our talk, he leaned back in his chair and said, "You know, if the president knew about your recommendations, he would order them to be done. The president," he continued, "is not afraid to take actions. Unfortunately, they'll never make it to his office. They," he said, pointing over his shoulder to the Pentagon, "will never let it get through the bureaucracy." He was right.

Nearly two years after the Beirut mission, other special operations experts were deployed to the Mediterranean in response to the hijacking of TWA Flight 847. The optimum moment for possible rescue slipped away, however, as the civilian and military sides of the Pentagon, the CIA, the State Department, and members of the National Security Council (NSC) tried simultaneously to debate and coordinate the effort. By the time anything approaching a consensus had been reached, the opportunity for a successful rescue attempt had long passed.

Shortly after the TWA 847 incident, the hijacking of the *Achille Lauro* again prompted a JCS order for the deployment of U.S. counterterrorist forces to the Mediterranean. Ultimately, it took 18 hours and 3 tries before the air force found a plane that could take the elite unit on its priority mission. By the time they reached the Mediterranean, it was too late to attempt an operation.

On a positive note, President Reagan did order strikes against Libyan targets in 1986 after intelligence indicated direct Libyan involvement in the bombing of a German discotheque frequented by U.S. soldiers. The nature of the raids, however, involved the use of conventional military forces in a general strike against Libya, not a counterterrorist strike against specific individuals who had been involved in terrorist activities.

When Rich Higgins's body was displayed on the front of newspapers, magazines, and television worldwide in 1989, there was an immediate outcry for swift retribution against those who had killed him. The Pentagon's response to media questions about retaliation was to state their concern that such strikes would endanger the lives of other hostages. In fact, the Pentagon had neither prepared plans nor updated target folders for any military actions against terrorist bases or sites in Lebanon. This is in direct contrast to the routine Pentagon procedure of maintaining and updating literally tons of plans and target folders against precise targets within the Soviet Union. Such precise targets also exist in Lebanon, but the Pentagon had long since ceased updating either plans or target folders, despite the long hostage drama and awareness that Lebanon continues to be a center of international terrorism.

Why do we seem so unable to strike effectively at terrorists? The issue of rescuing hostages—such as those being held in Beirut—or retaliating against terrorists are not always clear cut. All scenarios are quite different. A Beirut hostage rescue effort is much different from the rescue of hostages being held in an aircraft on the end of an airstrip or the rescue of an isolated hostage. A retaliation attack against a *Hezbollah* headquarters in Beirut's southern suburbs is different from an attack against a terrorist training camp in Lebanon's Bekaa Valley or a key military facility inside Iran. However, there are three principal elements that are common to all scenarios. The first is the need to have appropriately trained and equipped forces to conduct the mission. The second is the need for timely, accurate intelligence that can ensure a high probability of success. Finally, there is the need for key military and civilian leadership that can make the decision to deploy and then ensure adequate and proper support for the deployed force.

Consider first the question of whether the United States has the proper forces. Since the early 1980s, many expert studies have concluded that the United States is most likely to be challenged directly in ways that will not warrant the use of conventional or nuclear forces. As Defense Secretary Caspar Weinberger stated in his November 1986 speech outlining his six major criteria for the employment of U.S. combat forces abroad, the United States would have to consider "the consequences of failing to deter conflict at the lowest possible level," outside the spectrum of what the mainstream defense orientation has been.

It is, in fact, these unconventional threats posed at the lower end of the spectrum that have dominated U.S. military action during the past 10 years. Threats posed by terrorism, insurgency, and international drug trafficking are not generally suited to the employment of conventional forces. Rather, they are the domain of special operations forces, which have been organized, trained, and equipped to operate in a fashion different from that of their conventional counterparts. Each of the three services has its own dedicated special operations elements, and the Marine Corps has undertaken programs to provide special operations training to many of its units.

Since the end of the Vietnam War, no single U.S. military operation has had a more profound impact on the psyche of our nation than the failure of Desert One. Few Americans can forget the dismal scene on television screens and on the front pages of magazines and newspapers around the world—the wreckage of U.S. helicopters and a C-130 Hercules and the bodies of eight American soldiers strewn across the Iranian landscape. Some would argue that the failed hostage rescue effort will, for decades to come, influence the way the world views the ability of Americans to project their military power in engagements of limited scale.

The failure of Desert One quickly brought into question the ability of the United States to conduct special operations, and critics lost little time in recalling the failed prisoner of war (POW) rescue mission at Son Tay during the Vietnam conflict. (On November 21, 1970, a joint U.S. Army-

Air Force team had taken off from bases in Thailand, flown 400 miles to the Son Tay prison camp some 20 miles north of Hanoi, and raided the camp only to discover that the prisoners had been moved. The Americans killed 25 enemy soldiers and withdrew without loss.) Although the real culprit at Son Tay was faulty intelligence, the Son Tay mission was generally viewed as a special operations failure.

The other major special operations failure of the 1970s occurred in 1975 when U.S. Marine and Air Force elements attempted to rescue crewmen taken hostage from the U.S. merchant ship *Mayaguez* by Cambodian rebels. With inadequate prior planning, poor coordination, and no rehearsal, the rescue attempt turned into a debacle that had little influence on the ultimate release of the crewmen by the Cambodians.

Although Son Tay and the *Mayaguez* were failures, their impact paled in comparison to Desert One. In the aftermath of the failed Desert One operation, retired Admiral James L. Holloway chaired a prestigious panel of experts summoned to review all aspects of the operation and develop a comprehensive set of conclusions and recommendations. Key among the panel's conclusions was the fact that "by not utilizing an existing JTF [Joint Task Force] organization, the Joint Chiefs of Staff had to start, literally, from the beginning to establish a JTF, create an organization, provide a staff, develop a plan, select the units, and train the force before the first mission capability could be attained."

In 1980, the year of Admiral Holloway's report, the dynamics of U.S. military planning, contingencies, and operations did not dictate that an institutionalized structure be developed within the U.S. military to ensure the capabilities and readiness of special operations units or forces. Generally speaking, special operations forces served in supporting roles to senior commands, and only rarely undertook operations on their own. By the mid-1980s, however, as terrorism, insurgency, and other forms of unconventional conflict abounded, some of the dynamics of military force projection were clearly changing.

The June 1985 hijacking of TWA Flight 847 followed soon after by the hijacking of the *Achille Lauro* highlighted for the American public the glaring inability of the United States to respond decisively to acts of terrorism. And while the Pentagon languished in its conventional mentality, the Congress began to scrutinize the issue of military special operations forces.

The first major rounds from the congressional side were advanced in a series of articles in the *Armed Forces Journal* on special operations forces and possible ways to fix what was deemed broken. The first article appeared in August 1985 and was authored by Congressman Dan Daniels of Virginia, chairman of the Defense Readiness Subcommittee of the House Armed Services Committee. Congressman Daniels called for the creation of a sixth service—a special operations service. His piece noted, quite correctly, that congressional support for the issue was growing, that media attention was becoming intense and was generally favorable, and that public interest was intensifying. Although radical in nature, Congressman Daniels's ideas received quick support among reformists interested in special operations revitalization.

Coincidentally, the same *Armed Forces Journal* issue contained a small piece that noted that U.S. military forces had been unable to mount a hostage rescue attempt during the TWA 847 hijacking crisis because of a lack of available rotary wing assets.

In January 1986, Senator Bill Cohen of Maine authored an article in the *Armed Forces Journal* calling for the creation of a Defense Special Operations Agency. Like Congressman Daniels, Senator Cohen echoed many of the problems that faced the special operations community. Once again, also by coincidence, the same issue carried a piece noting that the air force's 1st Special Operations Wing at Hurlburt Field, Florida, had canceled an operational readiness inspection the preceding month when maintenance problems were encountered on all 11 aircraft scheduled for inspection. The problem, later reports indicated, was a lack of adequate spares to accomplish routine maintenance.

Shortly after Senator Cohen's article, the *Wall Street Journal* broke a story that the United States had been unable to get its counterterrorist forces off the ground during the *Achille Lauro* incident of the previous year. According to this article, "The Air Force plane assigned to carry them wasn't in shape to leave the country. After trying three planes, the SEALs [sea-air-land troops] finally took off, but they arrived after the terrorists had left the hijacked cruise ship, ending the hostage drama."

On May 15, 1986, Senator Cohen was joined by Senator Sam Nunn, chairman of the Senate Armed Services Committee, in introducing a bill into the Senate that called for a number of institutional changes to strengthen military special operations forces and, thus, the ability of the

United States to deal with low-intensity conflict. The following month, Congressman Daniels introduced his own legislation on the House side calling for a Defense Special Operations Agency similar to what Senator Cohen had called for in his January 1986 article.

In their own ways, both measures were considered radical. Congressman Daniels's bill would have established a chain of command that bypassed the Joint Chiefs of Staff and interposed a civilian between the military and the secretary of defense. The Senate version, although not removing the JCS from the chain of command, did represent the first attempt by Congress to establish a military command in law. Both measures were also striking, however, in that they demonstrated congressional interest in an area of the military that few even within the military itself understood and that had little or no constituency or political gain attached. Congress was clearly taking a leadership role in this unique area, a role that continues to this day.

Just after these congressional moves took place, in August 1986, the army released a study that had been commissioned to examine threats from the low-intensity conflict end of the spectrum. Reported on widely in the media, the study concluded that "as a nation we do not understand low intensity conflict; we respond without unity of effort; we execute our activities poorly; and we lack the ability to sustain operations." This candid admission, contained in the Joint Low Intensity Conflict Project Final Report from the army's training and doctrine command at Fort Monroe, Virginia, caught the immediate attention of Congress, keyed as it was to counterterrorism, counterinsurgency, and other conflicts that special operations forces had roles in.

Although the October 1983 invasion of Grenada had generally been viewed as a military success, congressional hearings in 1986 indicated that the employment of special operations forces had been misunderstood and mismanaged by senior military planners. In closed testimony before members of the Senate Armed Services Committee on August 5, 1986, the former commander of the Joint Special Operations Command (JSOC), Major General Richard Scholtes, testified that the Grenada operation was tailor-made for special operations forces. Seizing of airfields, striking at selected targets, and evacuating U.S. personnel was entirely within the scope and capabilities of JSOC's forces, but the Joint Chiefs opted for a plan that divided the action among the services. And, as General Scholtes noted, the integration of special operations forces into the overall plan was not well understood and poorly implemented by higher headquarters. Between October 21-24, JSOC's targets were changed nine times, and an attempt to get a pre-invasion JSOC reconnaissance element onto the island was turned down by the Joint Chiefs.

In addition to General Scholtes, other distinguished retired officers and Department of Defense (DOD) officials came before Congress in 1986 to express their views and concerns. The list included General Sam Wilson, General Edward "Shy" Meyer, General Bob Kingston, Noel Koch, and former CIA Director William Colby. They all spoke publicly in open testimony; many also worked behind the scenes with key congressional members and staffers to effect change.

As the deliberations in Congress continued, factions within DOD and JCS worked feverishly to forestall binding legislation. Chairman of the Joint Chiefs Admiral William Crowe and Assistant Secretary of Defense for International Security Affairs Richard Armitage testified before a House committee in early August 1986 that such legislation was not necessary and that the Pentagon would take its own steps to ensure that special operations forces received the attention that Congress wanted. However, in the view of those working the issue on the Hill, the Pentagon lacked sincerity.

During the time that Congress was considering whether or not the legislation should be binding, a key former Pentagon official came forward to express his views on the legislative deliberations. Noel Koch had held the office of principal deputy assistant secretary of defense for international security affairs for nearly five years and had retained responsibility for overseeing the revitalization of special operations forces, as well as for counterterrorism and antiterrorism matters. Koch sent a nine-page personal letter to one of the key Senate sponsors of the legislation. Among his arguments, he explained, "The cost of success we were able to achieve" in revitalizing special operations forces (SOF) "is not especially well known. It did not come easily, of course, and each step only seemed to harden the resolve of those in the uniformed services who have steadfastly opposed SOF to resist further progress. This resistance took many forms. Dishonesty was one of them."

The last attempt to forestall the pending legislation came in early October 1986 when then National Security Adviser John Poindexter entered the fray with a personal letter to key Senate and House sponsors of the legislation. Poindexter expressed the "President's concern over legislation now pending in the House and Senate that would require certain command arrangements for Special Operations Forces." In closing, Poindexter claimed that the plan that Admiral Crowe and Secretary Armitage were pushing represented "a responsible approach and should be allowed to proceed without interference."

In a biting response to the White House, Senator Warren B. Rudman, one of the legislation's key sponsors, wrote that "those of us who have followed this issue closely can only conclude that the 'too little, too late' response of the Administration is derived principally from Congressional initiatives."

Of the 15 findings that preceded the Senate bill, 5 bore directly on the issue of counterterrorism. They included

- that the threat to the United States and its allies from unconventional warfare, including terrorism and insurgency, continues to increase at an alarming rate;
- that the most likely use of armed force by the United States in the foreseeable future will be counterterrorist, counterinsurgency, and other unconventional operations;
- that conventional force commanders have a limited understanding of special operations force capabilities and have misemployed such forces;
- that the Department of Defense has not given sufficient emphasis to the planning and preparation for unconventional warfare missions or to the appropriate integration of special operations force capabilities into the national security strategy of the United States;
- that the Department of Defense has not given sufficient attention to ensuring the provision of adequate intelligence support for unconventional warfare missions.

In early October 1987, House and Senate conferees met to develop a final bill that would be acceptable to the sponsors and key supporters of the legislation. The final bill was based upon the individual bills that had been passed unanimously in both houses. Although the administration continued to lobby against any legislation, the conferees quickly reached agreement, and the legislation was passed as part of the Defense Authorization Act of 1987. Moreover, because of concerns that the president would veto the act for reasons not related to the special operations provision, the Congress took the unusual step of including the legislation in the Defense Appropriations Act of 1987.

Against the backdrop of strong congressional support, the final legislation as passed was simple and straightforward. In sum, it called for

- the establishment of a unified combatant command for special operations forces;
- the creation of an assistant secretary of defense for special operations and low-intensity conflict, with full responsibility for policy and resource oversight of special operations forces; and,
- the establishment within the NSC of a "Board for Low-Intensity Conflict" to coordinate the unconventional warfare policies of the Unites States.

In addition, the legislation recommends—although does not require—the establishment of the position of deputy assistant to the president for national security affairs for low-intensity conflict within the Office of the President.

Finally, because of concerns that one of the mechanisms the services and the DOD would use to neutralize the legislation would be budgetary, the legislation includes language that gives special operations its own major force program category.

The Pentagon responded to the legislation's passage by slowing its implementation. On the military side, the Pentagon delayed until the last possible minute before creating the mandated command and choosing the commander in chief (CINC). However, since the creation of the U.S. Special Operations Command (USSOCOM), headquartered in Tampa, Florida, the military side has accomplished many of the congressionally mandated and intended objectives.

In accordance with the legislation, all special operations force elements and commands stationed in the United States are now assigned to USSOCOM. Those forces assigned include army, navy, and air force elements of both the active and reserve force. Special operations units stationed overseas continue to be under the operational command and control of the theater CINC to which they are assigned, although the CINC of the USSOCOM retains certain responsibilities for those forces as noted below.

The legislation was specific about many of the functions that the CINC was to perform with respect to the special operations units coming under the CINC's command. Some of the mandated functions include developing strategic doctrine and tactics; training assigned forces; ensuring combat readiness; and, ensuring the interoperability of equipment and forces. All of these specific functions were designed to guarantee that forces would be capable, if called upon, to perform their unique role and mission.

For specialized counterterrorist operations, such as the rescue of hostages, the principal forces that the National Command Authority would call upon in most scenarios would come from the Joint Special Operations Command. JSOC was activated at Ft. Bragg, North Carolina, in 1981 following the failed Tehran rescue effort. JSOC has the publicly stated mission to "study the special operations requirements and techniques of all services to ensure standardization." However, JSOC's actual mission includes command and control, doctrine, training, and employment of DOD's principal counterterrorist forces, including the army's Delta Force, the navy's SEAL Team 6, and specialized aviation units of the air force's 23rd Air Force and the army's Task Force 160. As with other special operations units within the United States, JSOC reports to the CINC, USSOCOM, although provisions remain for other reporting chains during certain operational deployments.

Although many counterterrorist operations would be centered on JSOC capabilities and forces, other missions against terrorists might also include other elements of the special operations community to ensure a high probability of success. In fact, early planning for the TWA Flight 847 hijacking incident of 1985 included the use of Army Rangers to seize and secure Beirut International Airport and the use of U.S. Air Force special operations aircraft to insert certain counterterrorist elements against suspected hostage locations.

Of the three services, the army has traditionally had the largest share of special operations forces, led by its Special Forces Groups and its Ranger Regiment. In addition, psychological operations and civil affairs units are currently included within the army's special operations community because of the prime role they can play in low-intensity conflict scenarios.

The army's 1st Special Operations Command (1st SOCOM), activated at Ft. Bragg, North Carolina, in 1983, is the army's senior command, under which special operations forces are assigned. The mission of 1st SOCOM is to prepare, employ or provide, and sustain army special operations forces to conduct foreign internal defense, unconventional warfare, strategic intelligence, Ranger operations, strike operations, and related special operations in support of U.S. national objectives and military strategy in peace and war. The latter includes counterterrorist operations.

The army's Special Forces (SF) has four stated missions: unconventional warfare, foreign internal defense, direct action, and strategic reconnaissance. The Ranger Regiment's mission is "to plan and conduct special military operations in support of United States policy and objectives," and Ranger specialties are quick strike and shock action over short periods.

Within the navy, the Naval Special Warfare Command at Coronado, California, is the senior navy command for special operations units tasked and trained to conduct operations that are nonconventional and often covert or clandestine in nature. Such missions include the conduct of unconventional warfare; psychological operations; beach, coastal, and river interdiction; and certain special tactical intelligence functions normally applied in planning and conducting special operations in a hostile environment.

Navy special operations units include SEALs, special boat and swimmer delivery units, and special helicopter assets to support operations.

The air force's principal roles in special operations are to provide tactical air transport and heavy fire support. The 23rd Air Force, headquartered at Hurlburt Field, Florida, serves as the senior command for air force special operations units, which include specially equipped and highly capable aircraft. These aircraft include the Combat Talon, an MC-130 aircraft whose principal purpose is to conduct day and night infiltration, exfiltration, resupply, psychological operations, and aerial reconnaissance into hostile or enemy-controlled territory using air-land, airdrop, or surface-to-air recovery procedures. Combat Talon missions are normally flown at night, using the lowest possible altitude while over hostile territory at a ground speed of between 220 and 240 knots.

Very precise, specialized fire support is provided by the air force's AC-130 gunship, a basic C-130 modified with four side-mounted guns, including a 105 millimeter (mm) howitzer, and various sensors that make it very adaptable to a variety of special missions. Within permissive environments, it is especially effective in close air support (CAS), interdiction, and armed reconnaissance missions. It also has the capability of aiding in perimeter defense, escort, surveillance, search and rescue, infiltration/exfiltration, illumination, landing zone support operations, and a limited airborne command and control capability.   Special helicopter support is provided by the air force HH-53/MH-53 Pave Low, whose mission is to conduct covert day, night, or adverse weather infiltration, exfiltration, reinforcement, and resupply into hostile or nonhostile environments. The Pave Low's cruising speed is approximately 100 knots, and its unrefueled combat radius can range from 200 to 500 nautical miles depending upon its load.

In addition to the special operations forces and capabilities of the other services, the Marine Corps has conducted tailored training and equipping of certain afloat forces to ensure a unique forward-deployed special operations capability, which can provide timely response to certain critical requirements. Examples of missions these units can conduct include amphibious assaults of limited duration, acting as an advance force for a larger follow-on force, and providing an immediate response capability across a wide spectrum of contingencies by conducting special operations missions. The intention is not to duplicate the missions of other special operations forces, but rather to offer a complementary capability to existing special operations forces—one that is centered on the Marine Corps's established maritime role and mission.

In sum, it is appropriate to note that since the failure of Desert One in 1979 and, more specifically, since congressional initiatives of 1986, the U.S. military has undertaken a massive revitalization program to ensure the operational effectiveness of the special operations forces of the various services across a broad spectrum of mission requirements. Although Congress does deserve a large part of the credit, key advocates within the military structure, including the CINC, USSOCOM, have ensured steady progress toward the appropriate focus and resources for these units. And, although there were a few recorded problems in the employment of special operations elements in the 1989 Panama operation, on balance, their performance far exceeded that achieved under similar operational circumstances and conditions during the 1983 Grenada operation.

Given that the United States has capable forces, the next issue to discuss is intelligence. Because most special operations missions are high risk in nature, precise, detailed intelligence is generally a key requirement to success. The movement of a team into downtown Beirut to rescue a hostage would require excruciating details on the building they were to enter, the guard force that oversaw the hostage, the types of weapons and communications the guards had, the exfiltration route to safety, and a myriad other details necessary to ensure the operational plan's high probability of success. In contrast, special operations such as the strikes against Syrian antiaircraft positions, which shot down two U.S. Navy jets in December 1983, would not have required as much detailed intelligence for a successful mission because of their proximity to Beirut and because they were isolated targets, distant from innocent civilians. Nonetheless, adequate intelligence would have been a prerequisite to mission success.

The car bomb attack on the U.S. embassy in Beirut on April 1, 1983, was the first such terrorist act of its kind against a U.S. diplomatic facility. The road in front of the embassy was open to civilian traffic and, according to my own recollection, the embassy building itself was less than 100 feet from the road. No formidable security system was in place that could have precluded such an attack. Sixty-three people, including 17 Americans, were killed when the bomb exploded. Among those killed were some of the CIA's top experts on the Middle East, including Robert Ames who was visiting from the Langley, Virginia, CIA headquarters.

The attack was stark proof of the inadequacy of U.S. intelligence collection capabilities in Beirut, and the secretary of defense ordered a select military intelligence team to Beirut to perform a number of specialized missions, among them a review of intelligence support to the U.S. Marines deployed near the airport.

I was a member of that team, and during our short stay in Beirut we met with various U.S., allied, and Lebanese entities that either provided or had the capability to provide intelligence support to the Marines. Our meetings and interviews quickly made it obvious that significant intelligence existed, but that reporting, correlation, and analysis were not coordinated, thus causing gaps in review and dissemination. Accordingly, one of our recommendations dealt with a centralized intelligence support capability for the Marines, who were not augmented with the additional intelligence personnel and assets that their unique peacekeeping mission required, particularly in a hostile environment such as Beirut.

Unfortunately, as with the mission we undertook a few months after the bombing, our report was received with bland apathy in the Pentagon and at Marine Corps Headquarters. No one was willing to give serious consideration to the various recommendations aimed specifically at strengthening the intelligence posture of the Marines at the airport. Ironically, after the tragic bombing of October 23, 1983, all of the recommendations were ordered implemented immediately. And, as some who have studied the bombing have stated publicly, there is evidence that intelligence regarding the bomb and the Marines as a specific target was available, but was not given to the Marines.

Is Beirut an easy environment in which to collect intelligence? Not necessarily. The first time I went into Beirut, following the bombing of the U.S. embassy, all sectors of the city could still be entered by strangers. In the southern suburbs, however, where Amal and *Hezbollah* controlled their own areas, Westerners could travel, although with some discomfort.

When I returned four months later, following the bombing of the U.S. Marine Compound, it was not possible to travel into portions of the southern suburbs at all. A massive dirt berm had been erected around much of the sector, and armed checkpoints were located at all of the entrances. Inside the protection of the berm were those who had perpetrated the bombing of the Marine Compound.

In fact, for those who traveled between the downtown section of West Beirut, where the U.S. embassy was located, and the international airport, where U.S. forces were still headquartered, it was necessary to approach the main entrance to the southern suburbs before turning off to the airport. Both U.S. embassy and Marine policy required a minimum of two vehicles with appropriate weapons or guards and communications to make the journey. On an assignment such as we were on, we had to make the journey alone, and driving into the checkpoint area was always a very solemn, lonely endeavor. Although at that time no Americans had yet been taken hostage, more than 275 had been killed in attacks on the embassy and Marines, and it was disconcerting to approach the area with nothing more than the hope that all would be well.

In addition to the fact that the southern suburbs at that time were an area denied to overt traffic, there were still technical means of accomplishing intelligence penetration, and it was still possible to get close enough to the sector to have direct visibility of key targets from tall buildings bordering some of the suburbs' outer perimeter. The current situation in Beirut, however, is not as permissive, but viable intelligence opportunities still exist. In a fashion typical only of Beirut, each new round of fighting forges relationships among previously bitter enemies. As of this writing, the Lebanese army and *Hezbollah* have established a mutual dialogue, the result of factional fighting each has experienced with previous allies. And, each time new alliances are formed, no matter how tenuous, new intelligence opportunities develop.

It is no secret that U.S. intelligence collection capabilities about the groups holding the hostages is sorely lacking, in part because the United States has done such a poor job of penetrating their organizations with reliable agents and in part because the groups have become sophisticated in protecting themselves against these technical collection capabilities. Revelations about the capabilities of the National Security Agency to isolate telephone circuits, to voice print those talking over telephone lines, and to decipher diplomatic codes have not gone unnoticed by either terrorist groups or those states that provide their principal sponsorship. The result is that the United States must work harder to acquire appropriate intelligence operations or plan for or deploy forces in either rescue or retaliation missions.

Do current intelligence collection difficulties imply that we have always had these problems in Beirut? Not necessarily. In 1987, the *Miami Herald* ran a series of articles concerning the identity of those responsible for the 1983 bombings of the U.S. embassy and U.S. Marine Compound in Beirut. The *Herald's* stories not only specifically identified key individuals involved in the planning and execution of the bombings, but also details of the way Syria had provided logistical and technical support in the acquisition and preparation of the explosives. As subsequently reported, key White House officials confirmed the accuracy of the *Herald's* stories. Despite the detailed intelligence that was available shortly after the bombing, the United States refused to take retaliatory action.

In 1986, as a result of precise intelligence on the location of a number of the hostages being held in Beirut, detailed predeployment planning was undertaken by the military's principal counterterrorist forces in preparation for a rescue attempt. At the last moment, however, as the first intelligence operatives were about to be deployed, the White House ordered the mission scrubbed, allegedly because of the ongoing Iran-contra arms deals. Some individuals involved in this effort privately admit that the intelligence was precise and that a rescue attempt would have had a very strong likelihood of success.

Although current collection capabilities against terrorists or terrorist organizations in Beirut are extremely limited, exacerbated in large measure by the withdrawal of all official U.S. personnel from Beirut last fall, should the United States then eliminate rescue or retaliation as a viable planning option? I do not believe it should; nonetheless, it does provide a good excuse for those in the government who want to focus on release as the only option and quickly eliminates retaliation or rescue as secondary options. From a practical perspective, everyone would rather the hostages be released than rescued, but the underlying question is how long must they languish before a release can be negotiated among the diverse parties involved in their confinement?

The evidence indicates that the United States has the needed forces. There have been times when the United States has also had the intelligence. Why then has the United States not been able to act decisively? Perhaps because the weak link has historically been at the decision-making level. Why? There appear to be three interrelated elements at play when senior leadership has to make decisions regarding striking at terrorists—first, politics—that is, the risk and consequences of failure; second, a structure that has no experience or real understanding of the forces that would conduct such operations; and, third, a bureaucracy that does not allow for options to make their way to the president.

Consider first the question of politics. Retired Lieutenant General Sam Wilson is generally viewed as one of America's preeminent experts on military special operations. One of Merrill's Marauders during World War II, an early member of U.S. Army's SF, a former deputy director of the CIA, and director of the DIA, General Wilson has developed his own list of characteristics of special operations. Among them he notes that special operations, such as those that could be conducted against terrorists, are high risk/high gain, are strategic in impact and nature, and, as often as not, are directed by the National Command Authority. Because of the high visibility associated with the conduct of such operations, the risk to those ordering them to be undertaken is high. President Jimmy Carter's popularity rating plunged after the failed rescue attempt into Tehran. President Reagan's rating soured after the attack on Libya.

Although most of us would perhaps like to believe that political considerations are not of key importance when making decisions about how to deal with terrorists, it would be naive to believe they are not. From a practical perspective, no one wants to champion a special operations mission before the president only to have it fail. And, it is difficult to champion something that no one close to the president has real experience with.

This nation's top military and civilian leaders are products of the military experience that most U.S. soldiers have shared since before World War II—that of conventional forces. And that perception of the military influences their willingness, or lack thereof, to employ special units. No country in the contemporary world has had more success employing its special operations units than Israel. And, interestingly enough, within the Israel Defense Forces (IDF), every general officer has served at least one tour in special operations. In contrast, within the U.S. military, very few generals have served in special operations. And, it can be argued that their conventional perception of the military possibly influences their decision to employ special units.

When the planning for the attack on Libya was under way in the Pentagon, a series of recommendations for possible strikes against Libyan sites and facilities was provided by special operations. According to some who saw the recommendations, they were low risk, high gain, and none would have put innocent civilians at risk. However, the recommendations never received serious consideration by senior leaders in the Pentagon, and the options provided to the president instead centered on the employment of conventional forces against the targets.

Where then are the experts or advocates for these unique forces? When the Congress passed the 1986 special operations legislation, the Office of the Secretary of Defense (OSD) continued its opposition to the legislation by its approach to the new law's implementation. The first candidate chosen by Secretary Weinberger to be the new assistant secretary of defense for special operations and low-intensity conflict was on record as having opposed the legislation. The Senate Armed Services Committee refused to move his nomination forward, and the White House finally withdrew his name. When the Pentagon then delayed the nomination of a new candidate, legislation was passed mandating that Secretary of the Army John Marsh hold the position as a collateral duty until an appropriate candidate was nominated and approved by the Senate.

When Frank Carlucci became secretary of defense, he submitted a nominee who had no qualifications in either special operations or low-intensity conflict, but, by then, the Senate was tired of fighting the issue, and Carlucci's candidate was approved. Finally, when the Bush administration came to power, a former Senate Armed Services Committee staffer who had helped develop the legislation became the new assistant secretary. By then, however, the Pentagon had had enough time to build a wall around the Special Operations/Low-Intensity Conflict (SO/LIC) offices and the functions they were to perform. Accordingly, the work of the office progresses excruciatingly slowly, and promised support from higher Pentagon officials has not occurred.

In addition to the problems associated with filling key civilian positions within the Pentagon, the Reagan administration refused to appoint a deputy assistant to the president for low-intensity conflict. When the Bush administration came to power, key members of Congress weighed in quickly in an effort to encourage the president and National Security Adviser General Brent Scowcroft to fill this key position with an individual experienced in special operations and low-intensity conflict. Although an appointment was finally made, the individual selected did not have a strong background in either issue, and his designated responsibilities were diluted among four other issue areas.

Finally, this mixture of political concerns together with a lack of substantive special operations expertise at the highest decision-making levels allows the bureaucracy to keep rescue and retaliation options at some distance from the president. In addition, it fosters a "no one is in charge" environment on some of these matters. One of the intended results of the 1986 legislation was a strong NSC staff that could coordinate and oversee counterterrorist matters, advising the president directly. Instead, counterterrorism policy, planning, and responsibility continues to be spread among various agencies within the government, fostering frustration among many who want to see demonstrated leadership. As noted earlier, when Lieutenant Colonel Higgins was killed in 1989, there were no plans or target folders on the shelf that would have enabled even rudimentary efforts at striking back. Many continue to believe that the president is being shortchanged in these areas.

What, then, can be done? Should rescue and retaliation be rejected as viable options in dealing with terrorists? Most of us do not think so. Even in a changing world, it is unlikely that threats of terrorism against Americans or American interests will disappear in the near term. Accordingly, it would seem prudent that the administration undertake a few actions to ensure the president, and the American people, are better served on this matter.

One way to do so would be to identify the leadership within the administration on these matters. No one is in charge, but someone should be, and it would seem that the Congress was correct when it sought to institutionalize leadership at the NSC level. Someone needs to drive the interagency process to ensure that it works in a coordinated fashion, not permit agencies to go their own way based upon parochial interests. The intelligence situation in Beirut is difficult, but it becomes much more difficult when the CIA is unable to adequately support the CINC, USSOCOM, on his intelligence requirements, yet concurrently exercises veto authority over the conduct of military intelligence operations in Lebanon.

One outcome of effective leadership would be the development of contingency plans, appropriate policies, and operational doctrine that could guide the U.S. response to terrorism and terrorists. And, to the degree appropriate, such policies should be publicly stated to indicate U.S. resolve. At present, the United States' publicly stated policy is that it will not negotiate with terrorists, although it has done so. Perhaps there should be a publicly announced policy that when terrorists strike at the United States, the United States will respond directly against those terrorists or the states known to be supporting them.

Ironically, even after U.S. intelligence confirmed direct Syrian complicity in the bombing of the U.S. embassy and U.S. Marine Compound in Beirut, Syria retained its State Department's 'most favored nation status as a trading partner. Apologists in the State Department explained that allowing this was an effort to elicit more cooperation from Syria on the issue of terrorism.

A second step might be to review the recommendations of the report produced by a panel that President Bush chaired when he was vice president. According to knowledgeable sources, many of the recommendations contained in "The Vice-President's Report on Combating Terrorism" remain undone, in large part because individual agencies and departments refused to work together on the issues and, again, no one has exercised control or leadership.

Next, the administration should look to the leadership of such notables as retired Generals Sam Wilson, Ed "Shy" Meyer, Bob Kingston, and Paul Gorman, in directing a renewed focus on issues of rescue, retaliation, and the appropriate employment of special operations forces. Demonstrated expertise in the unique areas should be a prerequisite to advising the president on such matters. Without it, there can be no convincing argument that either the president or the American people are being well served.

Finally, one must ask, what are the consequences of failing to address these issues forthrightly? On a day-by-day basis, there are probably no consequences. However, acts of terrorism against Americans or American interests are not predictable. To this point, the visibility of the hostages in Beirut fluctuates from the back page to the front page on an infrequent basis. A protracted incident, such as that which occurred in Tehran, could quickly focus the attention of all Americans directly on how this and previous administrations have done. Many of us would have difficulty saying much has been done well.

2
Special Operations Against Terrorism: The Israeli Approach

Michael Eisenstadt

Few armed forces have compiled as impressive a record of success in the field of counterterrorism as the Israel Defense Forces. In Israel's case, necessity has provided the incentive for the development of a highly capable and sophisticated counterterrorist capability. Since the birth of the state in 1948, the threat of illegal border crossings by Palestinian Fedayeen irregulars, infiltrators, and refugees and, later, the threat of terrorism conducted by guerrillas belonging to the Palestine Liberation Organization (PLO) has been a pervasive fact of daily life. In addition, due to historical, cultural, and demographic factors and, as a result of the tight-knit nature of Israeli society, Israel is extremely sensitive to casualties. The trauma of losses suffered as a result of terrorism is felt on nearly all levels of society. Moreover, the constant threat of terrorism precludes the emergence of an atmosphere of normalcy in a country that has seen six major wars in little more than four decades. Finally, terrorism threatens Israel's deterrent capability. Israel invests substantial effort in cultivating and projecting an image of strength in order to deter its neighbors. Terrorist successes weaken this image. For instance, the spectacular airborne raid by two guerrillas belonging to the Popular Front for the Liberation of Palestine-General Command (PFLP-GC), who piloted two hang gliders across the Lebanese border and attacked an army base in northern Israel on the night of November 25, 1988, generated a sense of new-found pride and self-confidence among Palestinians that contributed to the outbreak of the Palestinian uprising (the *intifada*) in the West Bank and Gaza two weeks later.

The threat posed by terrorism has fostered the emergence of a national consensus concerning the desirability of a vigorous military response to the problem. Both Likud- and Labor-led governments have been susceptible to pressure from border development towns and kibbutzim that form important parts of their respective domestic constituencies and that have often borne the brunt of cross-border terrorist attacks. The IDF has also functioned at times as an institutional pressure group, and the chief of staff of the IDF and other senior officers have sometimes aggressively lobbied the minister of defense and other cabinet ministers for military action.

As a result of all these factors, nearly every Israeli government has devoted significant attention and resources to combating terrorism. In turn, this has spurred the development of a sophisticated counterterrorist capability through the creation a number of highly capable elite units in the ground and naval forces with counterterrorist duties.

The IDF's Counterterrorist Units

In the IDF, the counterterrorist role is fulfilled by several elite units capable of both conventional and special operations. Because the IDF embraces an offensive approach to counterterrorism, these units train to perform raids and reconnaissance missions, as well as more traditional counterterrorist missions such as hostage rescues.[1] These units receive high-level support from Israel's civilian and military leadership, as well as priority access to resources, including quality personnel, equipment, and intelligence support. This factor affects every aspect of the organization, training, and employment of these units and is a major factor in their success.

The IDF's elite units trace their origin to Unit 101, which was founded in August 1953 to carry out reprisal raids against Arab states harboring Palestinian Fedayeen and infiltrators. Its commander was Lieutenant Colonel Ariel Sharon, a battalion commander in the reserves. Although

Unit 101 numbered no more than 45 soldiers and carried out no more than a few dozen missions prior to its merger with the 890th Paratroop Battalion in January 1954, its legacy has influenced generations of IDF soldiers.

Unit 101 demonstrated that a small, elite unit could achieve impressive results on the battlefield and set the standards for and influence the performance of the entire armed forces. Moreover, the informal atmosphere, unique sense of esprit, and standards of combat leadership that characterized Unit 101 became standard norms for the IDF and part of the combat lore on which generations of IDF officers and enlisted men have been raised. Through the successors to Unit 101, its spirit has been perpetuated in the IDF.[2]

Primary responsibility in the IDF for counterterrorism is currently shared by five elite units: *Sayeret Matkal*, the General Staff Reconnaissance Unit; *Sayeret Tzanchanim*, the reconnaissance company of the 35th Paratroop Brigade; *Sayeret Golani*, the reconnaissance company of the 1st (*Golani*) Infantry Brigade; *Sayeret Giv' ati*, the reconnaissance company of the *Giv' ati* Infantry Brigade; and, *Kommando Yami*, the IDF's naval special warfare unit. The IDF may also possess a number of smaller, specialized units that may participate in the counterterrorist effort.[3]

Sayeret Matkal is the IDF's premier special operations unit. It is commanded by a lieutenant colonel and consists of about 200 soldiers (including staff and support personnel) organized into 10-12 man teams. It is subordinate to the director of military intelligence and is generally tasked with the most sensitive, dangerous, and demanding missions. Personnel have also reportedly been seconded to the *Mossad* to conduct assassinations. This unit is capable of insertion by sea, air, or land.[4]

Sayeret Tzanchanim, *Sayeret Golani*, and *Sayeret Giv' ati* are the reconnaissance companies of the IDF's three premier active infantry brigades. Each is commanded by a junior major or senior captain and consists of about 200 men (including staff and support personnel) organized into 12-16 man teams. They are capable of conducting conventional infantry and special operations independently or in conjunction with their respective parent brigades. They can also be inserted by sea, air, or land.[5]

Kommando Yami is the IDF's naval special warfare unit. It is commanded by a naval captain and consists of about 300 Naval

Commandos (including staff and support personnel) and is often tasked to conduct raids and reconnaissance missions against coastal targets. The unit also fulfills the at-sea counterterrorist role. Naval commando personnel also conduct beach reconnaissance and security tasks for paratroop and infantry reconnaissance units during seaborne insertions. The principal means of insertion employed by the Naval Commandos include armed speedboats, inflatable rubber rafts, swimmer delivery vehicles, submarine lockout, and swimming (surface and subsurface). Naval commando personnel are also capable of airborne insertion.[6]

Although the IDF's elite units can conduct counterterrorist operations independently, with little or no augmentation, the IDF will usually form, on a mission-specific basis, task forces comprised of ad hoc mission groups drawn from these units. Task forces are generally rank heavy, consisting of handpicked commissioned and noncommissioned officers, and the size and configuration of a task force and its constituent mission groups are mission dependent.[7] Task forces are also sometimes augmented by personnel possessing specialized expertise (such as intelligence, communications, and demolitions experts) from elsewhere in the IDF to create a mix of skills and capabilities not found in any single unit.

These units are among the finest within the IDF and act as centers of excellence that attract the best soldiers in the country. They provide intensive training and extensive operational experience to create a skilled and experienced leadership cadre. The IDF General Staff is dominated by former paratroop and infantry officers, many of whom have served in one of these units at some point in their careers. As a result, the IDF General Staff possesses a wealth of counterterrorism experience.[8] In addition, the IDF believes that these units encourage beneficial competition by setting standards of excellence that other units seek to emulate or surpass, thereby inspiring the spirit, enhancing the image, and raising the standards of the entire armed forces.

Although the employment of the IDF's elite paratroop and infantry units in the counterterrorist role in peacetime has generally proved satisfactory, these units are usually also employed as conventional infantry in wartime, and they therefore suffer the heavy casualty rates typically incurred by infantry. For instance, during the 1973 war, the *Golani* Brigade, with a total strength of about 2,500 men, suffered 440 casualties—130 deaths and 310 wounded, including the brigade's deputy commander, 2 battalion commanders, and the commander of *Sayeret Golani*. During the 1982 war in Lebanon, it suffered 46 deaths, including the commander of *Sayeret Golani* and 10 other *Sayeret* personnel.[9] As a result, its ability to fulfill its counterterrorist duties following both wars was significantly impaired.

Assessment and Selection of Personnel. The personnel selection process for the IDF's elite units is a key factor in their success. Selection commences prior to induction and continues through the initial phase of a soldier's compulsory service. The IDF attempts to identify potential candidates for its elite units at the earliest date possible. It employs a sophisticated array of screening physicals, psychological tests and interviews, aptitude tests, and questionnaires administered in the year preceding conscription and during the first week of active service. The tests are conducted to identify personnel possessing the requisite physical, psychological, and motivational attributes, leadership abilities, and special skills (such as proficiency in foreign languages) required by these units. Personal referrals from unit members may also play a role in selection.[10]

Candidates who score well on the pre-conscription tests are invited to volunteer for the IDF's most select elite units, such as *Sayeret Matkal* or the Naval Commandos and attend a mandatory pre-conscription assessment, known as *gibush* (or trials week), which lasts five days and tests their leadership skills, physical strength and endurance, and performance under stress. Subjective evaluations by unit personnel, in combination with objective test scores, serve as the basis for selection. Only about 10 percent of the candidates pass the *gibush Sayeret Matkal*, while about 30 percent pass the Naval Commando *gibush Kommando Yami*. Those who pass are offered the option of serving in these units upon conscription.[11]

By contrast, the 35th Paratroop, *Golani*, and *Giv'ati* Infantry Brigades do not conduct pre-conscription recruiting. The 35th Paratroop Brigade draws exclusively from volunteers at *bakum*, the IDF's absorption and assignment base at Tel HaShomer, near Tel Aviv, during the first week of service. Volunteers for the paratroops undergo a mini-*gibush* (or *gibushon*) at *bakum* lasting half a day, and only about 25 percent of all volunteers are accepted into the brigade, while the most promising candidates are offered the opportunity to volunteer for *Sayeret Tzanchanim*. They must pass a *gibush sayeret* lasting three days held at the Wingate Institute in Herzliyya, which consists of road marches, physical tests and trials, and leadership reaction drills. Only about 40 percent pass the *gibush sayeret*, and the best of these are selected for training as reconnaissance paratroopers. The remainder report for paratroop basic training and eventually serve in one of the line battalions of the 35th Paratroop Brigade. Volunteers for *Sayeret Golani* and *Sayeret Giv'ati* attend similar *gibushim* during their basic training.[12]

Finally, some personnel are identified on the basis of combat performance, peer ratings, and the recommendation of their commanders during the operational phase of their compulsory service. They may then transfer to one of these units as a noncommissioned or commissioned officer.

A mix of overt and latent incentives and pressures ensure that a high quality pool of applicants volunteer for service in elite units. The status and prestige accorded members of these units within the IDF and Israeli society at large is sufficient incentive for many to volunteer. In addition, service in elite units is considered a career enhancing move. Civilian employment opportunities may be more favorable for veterans of elite units, and service in an elite unit is perceived to be the fast track to the top for those planning a career in the military.

Training. Training for *Sayeret Matkal*, *Sayeret Tzanchanim*, and the Naval Commandos commences with paratroop basic training (*tironut tzanchanim*), which lasts six months, followed by airborne qualification. During the first weeks of basic training, conscripts are formed into teams (*tzevetim*) consisting of as many as 25 candidates. Each team member is assigned a specific role or functional specialization, such as rifleman, machine gunner, grenadier, sniper, radioman, or medic and receives specialized training, although emphasis is also placed on cross-training within the team. Training of team personnel is conducted by the unit chain of command—the team leader (a lieutenant) and team sergeant.

As a result of this arrangement, individual and collective training occur simultaneously, concurrently building individual and unit proficiency. Because individual training occurs within the team framework, it enhances unit cohesion and esprit. Conversely, collective training reinforces individual skills and proficiency and contributes toward a functionally integrated and cohesive unit. Unit performance is thus built on the foundation of collective and individual proficiency and unit cohesion.

Following paratroop basic training, candidates for *Sayeret Matkal*, *Sayeret Tzanchanim*, and the Naval Commandos continue with specialized training within the team framework, which is conducted by their parent units at various locations. Training emphasizes land navigation, combat marksmanship, demolitions, and communications, observing and reporting, camouflage and concealment, hand-to-hand combat, evasive driving, and infiltration and exfiltration techniques (including military free-fall parachuting). In addition, naval commando training emphasizes seamanship, underwater navigation, and scuba training. Attendance at a noncommissioned officer course is an integral part of qualification training for all these units and serve to hone the candidates' tactical and leadership skills.

Because of these requirements, the basic qualification courses for these units are very long. For example, a reconnaissance paratrooper in *Sayeret Tzanchanim* spends 20 months to qualify, and a Naval Commando spends 24 months. By the time a team finishes qualification training and commences operational service, its members have spent between 20-24 months training together, and, through attrition, its numbers have been significantly reduced. The product, however, is a tight-knit, cohesive, well-trained unit.

Nearly all officers in the IDF are selected from the ranks, and qualified reconnaissance and naval commando noncommissioned officers may attend an officer's candidate course (this entails an additional commitment of a year or more, depending on the unit). Although some newly commissioned second lieutenants return to their parent unit to train and lead teams of their own, others might be sent to fulfill positions elsewhere to help raise professional standards throughout the IDF. Those returning to their parent unit can expect to fulfill various command or staff positions and experience rapid advancement. This policy of continuous service within the same unit enhances unit cohesion and esprit and enables units to benefit from stability in the ranks and the experience of more senior personnel.

Mission Planning, Preparation, and Execution

The Plans Group. Because of the politically sensitive nature of special operations in general, and counterterrorist operations in particular, planning is generally conducted at the General Staff level. The planning process is characterized by the involvement of the most senior, capable, and experienced personnel in the IDF in all facets of the operation and by the close coordination among planners, intelligence personnel, and operators. This ensures the most effective utilization of available expertise, experience, and time; minimizes bureaucratic obstacles to effective communication and coordination; and ensures that intelligence is tailored to the requirements of the operators. The plans group is formed on an ad hoc basis and usually includes the chief paratroop and infantry officer and his staff, the commanders of the assault force, the chief of the operations branch of the General Staff and his chief of current operations, and the director of military intelligence. For joint operations, the commanders of the Israel Air Force (IAF) and Israel Naval Force (INF) and their key staff personnel, as well as key members of air and sea crews, are also included. In addition, the chief communications and electronics officer or the chief combat engineer officer may be included when special communications, electronic warfare, or engineering support is required.

The chief paratroop and infantry officer holds overall responsibility for planning and executing counterterrorist operations involving paratroop or infantry forces. He is also responsible for selecting units to participate in operations and for designating the assault force commander (who, in turn, selects the members of the assault force).[13] The commander of the Naval Commandos plays a similar role in planning and executing operations in which his unit plays the leading role. Although the chief paratroop and infantry officer is the key actor in the process of proposing, planning, and tasking counterterrorist operations, the entire process has traditionally been a highly competitive activity, involving a considerable amount of independent initiative and informal lobbying of the chief of staff and chief paratroop and infantry officer by the commanders of various elite units.

The chief of staff, moreover, is usually not directly involved in planning counterterrorist operations and generally provides only guidance and advice, although he may occasionally intervene to resolve interservice conflicts or other disagreements among planners. For instance, during preparations for a long-range naval raid on Palestinian bases in northern Lebanon on February 20-21, 1973 (Operation Hood 54-55), then Chief of Staff Lieutenant General David Elazar was forced to intervene to resolve a dispute between Chief Paratroop and Infantry Officer Brigadier General Emmanuel Shaked and Commander of the IAF Major General Mordechai Hod. According to Shaked, Elazar "ordered the commanders of the air force and the navy to place all the necessary means at my disposal, and he did so in a way that was absolutely unequivocal, so that we had a concerted effort....In this specific case, the chief paratroop and infantry officer was in charge of the operation, so everyone was at his service."[14] Nonetheless, a dispute arose between Shaked and Hod. According to Shaked

> I wanted [our troops] to be evacuated from a certain spot at the end of the operation, but the air force did not consider it appropriate for the landing of helicopters. After I had studied the terrain, together with my intelligence officer, I went to [the chief of staff] and said: "I believe that we have studied the subject more thoroughly than the air force, and an evacuation from [there] will make things much easier for us." Despite the fact that the professional officer in this case was none other than the commander of the air force and the issue was related to the air force, [the chief of staff] felt that the responsibility was mine and the thoroughness with which we had examined the question made my opinion worthy of acceptance.[15]

Although the involvement of the most senior and capable military personnel in the planning and execution of counterterrorist operations is a strength of the Israeli system, it may, in certain circumstances, also be a weakness. The most notable example occurred in September 1973, prior to the October 1973 war, when Palestinian terrorists belonging to the Syrian-sponsored al-Saiqa organization hijacked a train in Austria carrying Soviet Jewish émigrés. As a result of this action, Austria closed the principal transit facility for Soviet Jews at Schonau Castle. In the aftermath of this event, senior Israeli politicians were preoccupied with the ensuing political crisis with Austria, while the attention of senior military personnel and the intelligence community were directed toward the overseas terrorist threat—and not the emerging threat on Israel's borders, contributing to the success of the Egyptian and Syrian surprise attack several days later.

Intelligence Support. Detailed, accurate, and timely intelligence is vital to the success of counterterrorist operations. The direct involvement of the director of military intelligence and other senior intelligence personnel in the planning process ensures that counterterrorist task forces receive priority support from Israel's national level intelligence organizations, such as Military Intelligence and the *Mossad*. Intelligence support coordination lines are short and direct. The director of military intelligence or his deputy is a direct participant in the planning process and manages and coordinates the intelligence collection effort, thereby assuring unity of effort within the intelligence community. Moreover, the close coordination among intelligence and operations personnel (including members of the assault force itself) ensures that the intelligence collection effort and intelligence products are tailored to the needs of the consumers.[16] Conversely, intelligence personnel are frequently included in the task force to make on-the-spot evaluations of the intelligence value of captured personnel and documents, which may be brought back to Israel for interrogation or in-depth exploitation, respectively.

Responsiveness and Flexibility. The IDF believes that because of the inherent limitations and perishable nature of intelligence and because of the time pressures deriving from military considerations, it must be able to rapidly plan, prepare, and execute counterterrorist operations. As a result, it must be capable of improvising to react and adapt to the unexpected to accomplish a mission. For example, the Entebbe hostage rescue was planned, prepared, and executed within 48 hours. Speed and flexibility is enhanced by

- the IDF's willingness to allocate or divert resources and personnel from throughout the armed forces on a priority basis in support of an impending operation;
- the maintenance of mission folders for nearly every type of contingency and trained units capable of implementing them;[17]
- concurrent, parallel planning by all elements to make optimal use of available time.

In addition, the small size of Israel and the location of key units and facilities near the center of the country facilitates rapid planning and coordination.

Detailed Rehearsals. When feasible, rehearsals are conducted by using mock-ups or models of the target at locations in Israel resembling the area of operation. For instance, rehearsals for the storming of a hijacked Sabena Boeing 707 at Lod International Airport in May 1972 (Operation Isotope 1) were conducted on site with a Boeing 707 located in a nearby hanger. Similarly, rehearsals for the raid into Beirut in April 1973 to assassinate three senior PLO officials and destroy a Popular Democratic Front for the Liberation of Palestine (PDFLP) headquarters (Operation Spring of Youth) were conducted at an unoccupied residential apartment complex in north Tel Aviv that resembled parts of Beirut.

Rehearsals help test the validity of the concept of the operation, identify problems in its execution, hone techniques or special procedures needed, and improve the operational integration of the various elements involved in the mission. Plans are constantly refined and updated in accordance with insights gained during rehearsals and with the availability of new intelligence information until the time of execution. Like other aspects of the planning process, rehearsals are conducted concurrently by the various elements of the task force prior to a final rehearsal, which involves as many elements of the task force as is feasible.

Unambiguous Command Lines. Under Israeli law, cabinet approval is required for all military operations. However, counterterrorist operations generally attract particularly high-level interest and involvement because of the politically sensitive nature of these operations and the military risks involved. The defense minister often closely monitors the progress of an operation with the chief of staff, the chief of the operations branch, and other General Staff officers at the General Staff operations center ("the pit") at IDF General Staff Headquarters in Tel Aviv. However, once an operation commences, operational control is retained by the military. The chief of staff may occasionally enter the command net to offer guidance or advice, but the mission commander retains overall operational responsibility and decision-making authority. Command authority is usually limited to two principal echelons, and, as a result, command lines are clear, short, and direct:

- The mission commander is usually the chief paratroop and infantry officer. He reports to the chief of staff and has overall responsibility for the planning and execution of the operation. The mission commander is usually located at the General Staff forward command post, as close to the area of operations as possible—if necessary, aboard a naval vessel or aircraft.
- The task force commander has operational control of all assets dedicated to the mission and is the commander best able to assess and influence the situation. Several different individuals may fulfill

this role during successive phases of an operation, including the mission commander, the assault force commander, or the commander of air or naval assets transporting the assault force to or from the objective. However, the assault force commander usually fulfills this role during the assault phase of an operation.

This system preserves unity of command, while maximizing the operational autonomy and flexibility of the force commander and shortening the decision cycle, thus enabling the force commander to rapidly adjust plans in the event of unforeseen developments. This is vital because operations must sometimes be based on incomplete intelligence. Points left uncovered during planning can be resolved only at the discretion of the commander on the spot during execution. In addition, this system minimizes confusion about command relationships and simplifies communications to reduce net traffic, thereby diminishing the likelihood of a communications security breach.

Insertion. Israel's elite units are capable of insertion by sea, air, and land. For raids close to its border, overland approaches up to 15 kilometers (km) are preferred, with extraction usually accomplished by helicopter.

For reaching more distant inland objectives, the IDF has traditionally preferred the CH-53 heavy transport helicopter (and before that, the SA-321 Super Frelon) for the insertion of forces, due to its range, capacity, and reliability. During helicopter-supported operations, low-altitude flight profiles and terrain masking is employed to minimize the possibility of visual or radar detection, and air and artillery strikes on nearby targets are often employed as deceptive measures to draw attention away from the intended target and to mask the sounds of the approaching helicopters. Helicopters then insert the assault force out of the noise range of the objective (up to several kilometers away, depending on weather and terrain), and the objective is approached on foot, using terrain and stealth to mask the approach until the commencement of the assault.

Finally, the Mediterranean littoral offers particularly advantageous conditions for seaborne infiltration. The cluttered maritime environment in the Mediterranean hinders the identification and tracking of hostile surface ship movements, and thermal stratification and high ambient noise levels permit submarines to operate largely undetected throughout much of the area.

The INF maintains various assets that can be used for the insertion of counterterrorist forces. Its two Sa'ar 4.5 missile patrol boats can each accommodate two attack or medium transport helicopters, while its Reshef and Sa'ar III and II class missile patrol boats are capable of carrying inflatable rubber rafts and Bertram armed speedboats on side-mounted davits. The INF's three Type 206 Gal class submarines can insert personnel by lockout. Prior to a seaborne assault, Naval Commandos will generally be inserted under cover of darkness by a missile patrol boat offshore to reconnoiter and secure the landing site, followed by the assault force in rafts. Exfiltration is usually by raft or helicopter.

The range and flexibility of the INF's missile patrol boats was demonstrated by their role in the assassination of PLO leader Khalil al-Wazir in Tunis in April 1988. Two Sa'ar 4.5 and two Reshef-class boats reportedly transported a *Sayeret Matkal* assault force and a *Kommando Yami* security element to Tunis. Two AH-1S Cobra attack helicopters were reportedly aboard one of the Sa'ar 4.5s to provide fire support if necessary. An AB-206 was reportedly aboard the second Sa'ar 4.5 to provide on-call medical evacuation.[18]

The Importance of Surprise. The IDF conducts nearly all counterterrorist operations at night, under the cover of darkness, to maximize the likelihood of surprise and to exploit the IDF's operational experience and proficiency in night operations. Surprise is attained through secrecy, deception, and audacity.

Secrecy. The IDF's operations security (OPSEC) is generally excellent as a result of the elevation of secrecy to an institutional norm in the IDF, the adherence to conventional principles of OPSEC, such as compartmentalization and dissemination of information on a strictly need-to-know basis, and through the implementation of specific OPSEC measures, including

- the employment of dedicated OPSEC officers to monitor the security posture of units earmarked for an operation; measures include the monitoring of telephone calls and censorship of mail;
- the maintenance of routine patterns of ground and air activity to mask preparations for an operation;
- the observation of radio silence during the operation, except to provide specific instructions to the assault force in the event of

unforeseen developments, and to relay situation reports, using brevity codes whenever feasible; and
- strict censorship of military news reportage prior to, during, and after an operation.

In addition, investing the commander on the spot with responsibility for operational decisions and utilizing the command net primarily for reporting limits the volume of radio traffic and enhances the communications security of the assault force. Finally, the short planning time frame available for most operations minimizes the likelihood of an operations security breach.

Deception. To achieve surprise, the IDF employs a variety of deception techniques, including

- visual deception measures, such as the use of civilian clothes or foreign military uniforms, and foreign equipment and weapons by assault force personnel;
- passive and active electronic deception techniques, such as radar masking (shadowing civilian air and maritime traffic en route to an objective), and imitative and manipulative electronic deception and jamming of hostile radar to mask the presence or identity of IDF air or naval forces; and
- diversionary actions, such as air and artillery strikes in the vicinity of an objective to distract enemy radar operators and mask the sounds of helicopters used to insert the assault force near the object.

Audacity. The IDF believes that there is a direct relationship between audacity and success in counterterrorist operations. The deeper one strikes into hostile territory, the greater the likelihood of achieving surprise and the greater the psychological effect on the enemy. In the words of former Chief Paratroop and Infantry Officer Emmanuel Shaked, who played a central role in the emergence of Israel's particular approach to special operations: "I always believed...that an operation 200km from the border is less dangerous than an operation near the border, since surprise is assured."[19] As a result, the IDF has tended to favor hitting the enemy deep in its own territory and has developed an impressive capability for long-range operations.

Throughout the years, however, many of the IDF's finest soldiers have been killed in counterterrorist operations, and following the costly 1982 war in Lebanon and its messy aftermath, the IDF has been reluctant to employ these units in high-risk actions that could be accomplished by the air force or by other means.

After-Action Reviews. After-action reviews are held immediately after every operation and are used to evaluate the planning, preparation, and execution to derive lessons learned. Participants include members of the General Staff and the task force. The review is usually held at the General Staff forward command post. Participants are expected to be direct and honest in their reporting, without deference to rank, and the informality that characterizes relations between ranks in the IDF generally encourages candor. These are followed by more thorough and detailed after-action reports based on internal post-mission debriefs conducted at the various levels of command of all elements involved in the operation. In addition, a staff historian from the IDF chief historian's office is usually present during the operation as an observer at the General Staff forward command post. After observing and taking notes on the operation from this privileged vantage point, the historian will later publish a comprehensive account of the operation base on post-mission debriefs, after-action reports, message traffic, taped transcripts of radio voice communications, photographs, and interviews with participants.

Conclusion

For a variety of reasons, Israel's political and military leadership has provided strong support to its counterterrorism effort. This fact influences every aspect of the organization, training, and employment of the IDF's elite units, and is a key factor explaining their success.

Senior IDF personnel generally recognize, however, that no single military operation or success can solve the problem of terrorism. Many believe that within the context of a protracted conflict, special operations against terrorism may yield benefits by degrading the offensive military capabilities of terrorist organizations, disrupting their operational planning and activities, eliminating key personnel, inflicting casualties, destroying military facilities and equipment, and forcing them to allocate additional resources to self-defense and security.

As a result, as long as the threat of terrorism exists, Israel will continue to carry out special operations as part of its counterterrorism effort due to its belief in the military efficacy of these operations, and their beneficial effect on Israeli morale.

APPENDIX: Three Counterterrorist Operations

The Shores of Tripoli: Operation Hood 54-55 (February 20-21, 1973)

Operation Hood 54-55—a seaborne raid on PLO facilities near the northern Lebanese port of Tripoli on the night of February 20-21, 1973—was the IDF's first large-scale joint operation involving all three services and, until the assassination of PLO chief Khalil al-Wazir in Tunis in April 1988, the longest seaborne raid ever conducted by the IDF.[20] The two-pronged raid was conducted by six separate mission groups against seven separate targets located in the Nahr al-Barid and Al-Badawi refugee camps north of Tripoli.

Following the receipt of precise intelligence concerning PLO facilities in Nahr al-Barid and Al-Badawi, Chief of Staff Lieutenant General David Elazar asked Chief Paratroop and Infantry Officer Brigadier General Emmanuel Shaked on February 16 to plan a raid against them. Because of weather, light, and tidal conditions, the operation was scheduled for the night of February 20-21, leaving Shaked only four days to plan and prepare.

The plans group consisted of Shaked, Colonel Uzi Ya'iri (commander of the 35th Paratroop Brigade), and representatives of the operations and intelligence branches of the General Staff, and the navy and air force. The plan they developed called for the assault force to be divided into two separate task groups, which would be inserted near the objectives by missile patrol boats and infiltrate ashore in rubber rafts, followed by an overland approach and simultaneous assault on the two main clusters of objectives in Nahr al-Barid and Al-Badawi. Afterward, both task groups would be extracted by helicopter. Shaked would oversee the operation from a missile patrol boat offshore.

Because of the distance separating the two main objectives, the assault force was divided into two separate task groups. The task group assaulting the Al-Badawi camp (Hood 55) was led by Colonel Ya'iri, and consisted of three mission groups:

- *Force A*, led by Lieutenant Colonel Amnon Shahak, a battalion commander in the 35th Paratroop Brigade, consisted of 24 paratroopers tasked to demolish an al-Fatah training base and workshop. The guerrillas fled after hearing the initial volley of gunfire, and Shahak and his men collected documents and demolished the main buildings.
- *Force B*, led by Lieutenant Colonel Mula Shaham, a battalion commander in the 35th Paratroop Brigade, consisted of 26 paratroopers tasked to raid a Popular Front for the Liberation of Palestine (PFLP) base and prison. Following close-quarters combat in which 18 guerrillas were killed (the force suffered no casualties), Force B demolished most of the buildings at the base.
- *Force C*, led by Captain Avner Hermoni, commander of *Sayeret Tzanchanim*, consisted of 16 reconnaissance paratroopers tasked to assault an al-Fatah regional headquarters and armory. Following violent close-quarters combat in which Hermoni and three of his men were wounded, the force withdrew from the headquarters building. However, a secondary force succeeded in demolishing the armory.

The task group assaulting the Al-Badawi camp (Hood 54) was led by Lieutenant Colonel Amos Yaron, deputy commander of the 35th Paratroop Brigade, and consisted of three mission groups:

- *Force A*, led by Lieutenant Colonel Yitzhak Mordechai, a battalion commander in the 35th Paratroop Brigade, consisted of 24 paratroopers tasked to assault a naval base operated by al-Fatah. After silencing the base's two sentries and demolishing its gate with Bengalore torpedoes—and a brief but violent firefight in which 14 guerrillas were killed, 1 captured, with no losses to the force—Force A seized dozens of documents, maps, and photos before demolishing the building.
- *Force B*, led by Major Doron Rubin, commander of the 35th Paratroop Brigade's squad leader's course, consisted of a mixed group of paratroopers and Naval Commandos tasked to demolish a

Popular Struggle Front headquarters building. In a brief firefight, three guerrillas were killed and the building was then demolished (four members of the force were injured when a grenade tossed by a naval commando bounced off metal grillwork on a window, rolled back, and exploded).

- *Force C*, led by Lieutenant Commander Gadi Shefi, a senior naval commando officer, consisted of Naval Commandos, and was tasked to demolish a headquarters of the PFLP. Finding the building empty, they demolished it after searching for documents.

Except for some minor glitches, the operation was implemented almost exactly as planned and was a major success: 37 guerrillas were killed, 65 were wounded, and 1 was captured. Five bases were destroyed and two heavily damaged, while numerous documents, maps, and photos of intelligence value were seized. Only eight Israelis were wounded. In addition, beyond its immediate military impact, Operation Hood 54-55 provided the inspiration for an even more daring and spectacular raid on Beirut two months later (Operation Spring of Youth, April 9-10, 1973).

Into the Heart of Beirut: Operation Spring of Youth (April 9-10, 1973)

Operation Spring of Youth—a multipronged raid in Beirut and Sidon—was one of the most complex and successful long-range raids ever mounted by the IDF.[21] The operation was carried out simultaneously by five independent mission groups against eight separate objectives in and around Beirut and Sidon. It marked the culmination of an 18-month struggle between the PLO and the Israeli intelligence services, which included hijackings, assassinations, and letter and car bombings, and was the largest and last major counterterrorist operation launched by the IDF prior to the 1973 war.

The inspiration for the Beirut raid was provided by precise intelligence concerning the life-style and routines of several senior PLO officials collected by *Mossad* agents in Beirut. Moreover, the success of Operation Hood 54-55 convinced Chief of Staff Lieutenant General David Elazar and Chief Paratroop and Infantry Officer Brigadier General Emmanuel Shaked that a similar operation against PLO facilities in Beirut was possible. Planning commenced for an operation to assassinate three senior

PLO officials and demolish a headquarters of the Popular Democratic Front for the Liberation of Palestine, along with several supporting diversionary raids against various secondary objectives on the outskirts of Beirut and in the south of Lebanon.

Several days prior to the operation, six *Mossad* agents traveling under false European passports arrived separately in Beirut to make last minute arrangements and rent six cars that would be used by two of the mission groups.

On the night of April 9-10, 1973, a task force of nine Sa'ar class missile patrol boats and two Dabur class patrol boats departed from Haifa and inserted five mission groups in rubber rafts at various points off the Lebanese coast. Mission commander, Brigadier General Emmanuel Shaked and his command group were located on a missile patrol boat off the shore of Beirut, while the chief of staff and defense minister, located in the General Staff operations room in Israel, monitored the radio traffic throughout the operation.

The timing and location of the insertion were fixed to facilitate the near-simultaneous arrival of the various mission groups at their respective objectives to confuse Lebanese and Palestinian forces concerning the scope and focus of the attack. Naval Commandos secured the various landing sites prior to the landing and the withdrawal of the forces. The various mission groups and objectives were as follows:

- *Force A* was led by Lieutenant Colonel Ehud Barak, commander of *Sayeret Matkal*. It consisted of between 16-18 reconnaissance paratroopers from *Sayeret Matkal* and was tasked to assassinate three senior al-Fatah officials—Muhamad Yusuf al-Najjar (head of al-Fatah's Black September organization), Kamal Adwan (al-Fatah's chief of operations), and Kamal Nasir (spokesman for al-Fatah)—that lived in two adjacent apartment buildings in the Ramlat al-Beida district of West Beirut. After coming ashore, Barak's force was picked up by three waiting automobiles driven by *Mossad* personnel and taken to their objective. While a security element remained at the entrance of the two buildings, Barak's men broke up into three groups of 5-6 men each and went upstairs into the two buildings, killed the three al-Fatah officials, and gathered documents from their apartments. The operation lasted about 20 minutes in all. As Barak's force departed, three land-rover jeeps of Lebanon's gendarmerie arrived, and one that attempted to interfere with their departure was riddled with bullets.

- *Force B* was led by Lieutenant Colonel Amnon Shahak, a battalion commander in the 35th Paratroop Brigade. It consisted of 14 men divided into 3 elements and included reconnaissance paratroopers from *Sayeret* Tzanchanim and engineer-sappers from the 35th Paratroop Brigade's engineer company. It was tasked to raid and demolish a barracks and headquarters of the PDFLP near the Sabra refugee camp in West Beirut. After coming ashore, Shahak's force was picked up by three waiting automobiles driven by *Mossad* personnel and taken to their objective. Following bitter close-quarters combat during which numerous PDFLP guerrillas were killed and wounded, and three soldiers in Shahak's force were severely wounded, his men succeeded in fixing demolition charges to the foundation of the building. They withdrew to the beach 24 minutes after having commenced operations.
- *Force C* was led by Deputy Chief Paratroop and Infantry Officer Colonel Shmuel Pressberger and consisted of a force of Naval Commandos. It was tasked to demolish an al-Fatah workshop that produced naval mines and demolitions and an ammunition cache, located on the northern outskirts of Beirut. It accomplished its mission without any losses.
- *Force D* was led by Captain Shmuel Ziv, a senior naval commando officer, and it was composed of Naval Commandos. It was tasked to demolish an al-Fatah headquarters responsible for operations in Gaza, and an al-Fatah ammunition factory, located in the southern suburbs of Beirut. It accomplished its mission without any losses.
- *Force E* was led by Colonel Uzi Ya'iri, commander of the 35th Paratroop Brigade. It consisted of *Sayeret Tzanchanim* reconnaissance paratroopers and was tasked to demolish an al-Fatah garage and vehicle repair facility north of Sidon. It accomplished its mission without any losses.

In all, about 40 Palestinians and 4 Lebanese were killed, while several PLO facilities were demolished. The IDF suffered three casualties, including two killed. The raid was a spectacular success. It shocked the PLO's leadership, which had previously believed that it was secure in Beirut. Information derived from captured documents was instrumental to the arrest of a number of PLO operatives in Israel, the West Bank, and Gaza.

Fifteen years to the week after Operation Spring of Youth, the IDF conducted a nearly identical operation when two Sa'ar 4.5 and two Sa'ar 4 missile patrol boats transported a *Sayeret Matkal* hit team to Tunisia to assassinate the head of the PLO's Western Sector apparatus, Khalil al-Wazir (*Abu Jihad*) at his seaside villa near Tunis. After Naval Commandos secured the beach, about 40 *Sayeret Matkal* personnel in rubber rafts landed ashore under cover of darkness and proceeded to link up with several waiting *Mossad* personnel. They then proceeded to al-Wazir's residence in several rented cars. While the Mossad drivers waited in the cars and several members of the assault force provided security outside *Abu Jihad's* villa, an eight-man force broke into his residence and proceeded to his bedroom, where they killed him in his bed. Meanwhile, an IAF Boeing 707 command post with Deputy Chief of Staff Major General Ehud Barak aboard orbited offshore and monitored the conduct of the operation, while a second 707 jammed communications to and from al-Wazir's residence. The assault force then returned to the beach, where they linked up with waiting Naval Commandos and exfiltrated by raft to the missile patrol boats waiting offshore.

Rescue at Entebbe: Operation Yonatan
(July 3-4, 1976)

Operation Yonatan—the Israeli airborne rescue of 104 hostages held by Palestinian and German terrorists at Entebbe Airport in Uganda—was one of the most spectacular and successful counterterrorist operations ever carried out by the IDF.[22] On June 27, 1976, an Air France airbus flying from Tel Aviv to Paris via Athens was hijacked by terrorists affiliated with the Popular Front for the Liberation of Palestine-Special Operations Group of Dr. Wadi Haddad. The hijacked aircraft flew by way of Benghazi, Libya, to Entebbe Airport, Uganda.

With the arrival of the aircraft and the hostages in Uganda, informal preliminary planning for a rescue commenced among several independent staff elements. The plan eventually adopted called for a nighttime combat assault by a large joint task force consisting of at least five elements: a command group, a communications group (collocated with airborne elements of the command group), an assault force, an air force refueling team (which was integrated into the assault force), and a medical aid group. It was transported to the objective aboard four C-130 Hercules transport aircraft. In addition, two specially modified Boeing 707s served as a flying command post and a makeshift field hospital. The flying command post orbited the airport throughout the operation and provided a communications link with the chief of staff and Israel's senior political leadership, while the field hospital waited in Nairobi, Kenya, for casualties.

The assault force—which was selected by Brigadier General Shomron—consisted of more than 200 men and was organized into four elements:

- *Force A*, the primary assault force, was led by Lieutenant Colonel Yonatan Netanyahu, commander of *Sayeret Matkal*. It consisted of reconnaissance paratroopers from *Sayeret Matkal*, dressed in Ugandan army type uniforms, a black Mercedes limousine, and two land-rover jeeps (to simulate Idi Amin's entourage). Located in the first aircraft, it was tasked to storm the old terminal building, where the hostages were held.
- *Force B* was led by Colonel Matan Vilnai, commander of the 35th Paratroop Brigade. It consisted of reconnaissance paratroopers from *Sayeret Tzanchanim* located in the first and second aircraft and an air force refueling team, located in the fourth aircraft. It was tasked to storm the new terminal building, seize the refueling facilities and the new control tower, and secure and illuminate the runway with portable beacon lights emplaced by two teams located on the first aircraft.
- *Force C* was led by Colonel Uri Sagi, commander of the *Golani* Infantry Brigade. It consisted of reconnaissance personnel from *Sayeret Golani*, and a Peugeot pickup truck for casualty evacuation, located in the third and fourth aircraft. It was tasked to serve as a reserve for Force A in the event that it should experience difficulties and to assist in the evacuation of the hostages to a waiting aircraft.
- *Force D* was led by Major Shaul Mofaz, a senior officer in *Sayeret Matkal*. It consisted of reconnaissance paratroopers from *Sayeret*

Matkal and four BTR armored personnel carriers, located in the second and third aircraft. It was tasked to isolate the old terminal building and assist in the evacuation of the hostages.

A medical aid group headed by Dr. Eran Dolev consisting of combat surgeons and medics was located in the third and fourth aircraft and the modified Boeing 707 field hospital that landed in Nairobi.

Following a series of rehearsals, the task force took off from the IAF base at Ophira in the Sinai at 15:30 on July 3, less than 48 hours after formal preparations for the operation had commenced and prior to receipt of government approval for the operation. Cabinet authorization was eventually received in flight. The aircraft flew low over the Red Sea to avoid detection by radar.

At 23:01, only 30 seconds behind schedule, the first C-130 landed at Entebbe immediately behind a British civil transport flight to maximize the likelihood that the runway lights would be on and to mask the approach of the aircraft. The primary assault force then exited the rear of the aircraft and stormed the old terminal building, achieving nearly total surprise and killing all the terrorists. The assault on the old terminal building took approximately 15 seconds and was completed within 3 minutes after the lead C-130 had landed. The remainder of the operation was executed almost precisely as planned. At 23:52, the C-130 carrying the freed hostages took off, and by 23:59, the last element on the ground departed. The task force stopped at Nairobi airport in Kenya to refuel. At this time, one casualty was transferred to the hospital Boeing 707, and two others were taken to hospitals in Nairobi for emergency treatment. The aircraft then continued on to Israel.

The operation was a spectacular success. Casualties included 3 hostages killed, 5 wounded, 1 member of the assault force (its leader Lieutenant Colonel Netanyahu) killed, and 4 others wounded, and all 13 terrorists killed. About 35 Ugandan soldiers were also killed during the operation and 8 Ugandan MiG-17s and -21s were destroyed on the ground. The operation constituted one of the IDF's greatest victories against terrorism and helped restore Israel's self-confidence and refurbish the image of the IDF in the traumatic post-1973 war period.

Notes

1. By comparison, in most armies, the counterterrorist role is fulfilled by highly specialized, dedicated hostage rescue units, reflecting a largely defensive, reactive approach to the problem.

2. The philosophy guiding the funding of Unit 101, and subsequent elite units in the IDF, was succinctly summarized by Ariel Sharon in a recent interview: "I am a follower of the system that says that every army must have a small elite unit. As soon as there is such a unit, all the other units will work to raise their standards. If you look closely, you will see that the accomplishments of the special unit later become standard fare for the rest of the army and that the special unit progressed even further." Hanoch Scheinman, "101 Now: Sharon Remembers," *Bamahane*, October 2, 1985, pp. 19-21, translated in *Joint Publication Research Service Report, Near East and South Asia*, January 9, 1986, p. 63.

3. The Israel Border Guard also has a special counterterrorist unit, *Yamam* (*Yechida Neged Michablim*), which has competed with the various military units for recognition and a greater role in the counterterrorist effort. Established in May 1974, the unit has reportedly provided support to the *Shin Bet* (Israel's civilian internal security intelligence service) during cordon and search operations in Israel, the West Bank and Gaza, and southern Lebanon. In its first major operation, it rescued a busload of Israelis taken hostage by Palestinian guerrillas near Dimona, Israel, in March 1988. See Leroy Thompson, *The Rescuers: The World's Top Anti-Terrorist Units* (Boulder, Colo.: Paladin Press, 1986), 131-132; Topaz Carmi, "We Proved Our Worth," *Bamahane*, September 22 1988, p. 9. In addition, since 1988, the IDF has established a number of snatch squads, reportedly composed of personnel who speak Arabic and dress as locals and operate in the West Bank and Gaza to identify and apprehend leaders of the Palestinian uprising. Two of these units—code named "Samson" (*Shimshon*) and "Cherry" (*Duvdevan*)—achieved a certain degree of international notoriety following accusations in the Western press that they were engaged in the assassination of Palestinian activists. See Jon D. Hull, "Code Name 'Cherry,'" *Time*, November 7, 1988, p. 41.

4. Christopher Dobson and Ronald Payne, *Counterattack: The West's Battle Against the Terrorists* (New York: Facts on File, Inc., 1982), 77-93; Uri Milstein, *History of the Paratroops: Spring of Youth*, in Hebrew (Tel Aviv, Shalgi Publishing, 1987), 1545-1550.

5. Rami Carmel, "To Be a *Sayeret* Trooper," *Soldier of Fortune*, April 1989, p. 43.

6. Milstein, *History of the Paratroops*, 1421-1463; Haim Ravia and Emanuel Rosen, *So You've Been Drafted!* in Hebrew (Jerusalem: Keter Publishing House, 1989), 147-148.

7. For instance, Chief of Staff Lieutenant General Dan Shomron, a former chief paratroop and infantry officer commanded the hostage rescue at Entebbe in July 1976. Deputy Chief of Staff Major General Ehud Barak, a former commander of *Sayeret Matkal*, participated in a number of major counterterrorist operations, including Operation Isotope 1, the rescue of hostages aboard a hijacked Sabena airliner at Lod International Airport in May 1972, and Operation Spring of Youth, the assassination of three senior PLO officials in Beirut in April 1973. Director of Military Intelligence Major General Amnon Shahak, a former battalion commander in the 35th Paratroop Brigade led the assault on PDFLP headquarters in Beirut during Operation Spring of Youth. Ground Corps Commander Major General Uri Sagi, a former commander of the *Golani* Infantry Brigade and *Sayeret Golani*, led the *Golani* contingent at Entebbe. Commander of the IDF Southern Command Major General Matan Vilnai, a former chief paratroop and infantry officer and commander of the 35th Paratroop Brigade and *Sayeret Tzanchanim*, led the paratroop contingent at Entebbe. Commander of the IDF Central Command Major General Yitzhak Mordechai, a veteran of the 35th Paratroop Brigade, participated in Operation Hood 54-55, the seaborne raid on Palestinian bases in northern Lebanon in February 1973. And Chief of the General Staff Training Department Major General Doron Rubin, another veteran of the 35th Paratroop Brigade, participated in Operation Hood 54-55 and commanded the daring IDF raid on al-Na'imeh, near Beirut, in December 1988.

8. Casualty figures for the 1973 war are from Avi Bettelheim, *Golani: The Fighting Family*, in Hebrew (*Golani* Brigade Command, July 1980), 166. Casualty figures for the 1982 war cover only the period June 6-26, 1982, and are from Avi Bettelheim, *Golani in Peace for Galilee*, in Hebrew (*Golani* Brigade Command, October 1982), 62-63.

9. Mission groups from *Sayeret Tzanchanim, Golani*, or *Giv'ati* are often augmented by personnel from the line battalions and the combat engineer companies of their respective parent brigades.

10. The IDF believes that these tests and evaluations provide a reliable, predictive index of performance and professional success. For additional details, see Reuven Gal, *A Portrait of the Israeli Soldier* (New York:

Greenwood Press, 1986), 76-96; Ravia and Rosen, *So You've Been Drafted!* 11-74.

11. The Naval Commandos also conduct a pre-conscription *gadna* (paramilitary youth) scuba course during summer vacation. Those who pass the course are offered the option of serving in the unit. Ra'anan Tchervinsky, *Mommy, or the Commandos,* in Hebrew, *Ben Galim,* December 1986, pp. 36-38; Ravia and Rosen, *So You've Been Drafted!* 20-21.

12. Ibid., 98-99; Dor'am Gunt, *Everyone Wants Sayeret,* in Hebrew, *Bamahane,* March 22, 1989, pp. 19-20.

13. In peacetime, the chief paratroop and infantry officer heads the paratroop and infantry branch of the IDF's Ground Corps Command and is responsible for organizing, training, and equipping all paratroop and infantry forces in the IDF, for developing doctrine for their employment in wartime, and for preparing them for combat.

14. Hanoch Bartov, *Dado: 48 Years and 20 Days* (Tel Aviv: Ma'ariv Book Guild, 1981), 173.

15. Ibid.

16. The fact that five of the last six directors of military intelligence— Major Generals Amnon Shahak (1986-present), Ehud Barak (1983-1986), Shlomo Gazit (1974-1979), Eliahu Zeira (1972-1974), and Aharon Yariv (1963-1972)—had combat arms backgrounds in paratroop or infantry units and, in most cases, extensive operational counterterrorist experience probably accounts in part for the high quality of intelligence support for counterterrorist operations.

17. According to former Chief Paratroop and Infantry Officer Brigadier General Emmanuel Shaked, "[There is] a mission folder for every type of operation and the moment that there is sufficient intelligence, I am able to pull the folder and execute." Milstein, *History of the Paratroops,* 1604.

18. David Halevy and Neil C. Livingstone, "The Killing of *Abu Jihad,*" *The Washingtonian,* June 1988, p. 166.

19. Milstein, *History of the Paratroops,* 1604.

20. Sources used for constructing this account include: Colonel Yehuda Wallach, Moshe Lissak, and Arieh Itzchaki, eds., *Carta's Atlas of Israel: The Third Decade, 1971-1981,* in Hebrew (Jerusalem: Carta, 1983), 39; Milstein, *History of the Paratroops,* 1601-1612; Yosef Argamon, *Operation Hood,* in Hebrew, *Bahamane,* February 24, 1988, pp. 1616-1618, 1647; Samuel M. Katz, *Follow Me! A History of Israel's Military Elite* (London: Arms & Armour Press, Ltd., 1989), 109-111.

21. Sources used for constructing this account include: Uri Dan, *The Finger of God*, in Hebrew (Ramat Gan: Masada Press, 1976), 106-125; Ilan Kfir, *Israel Defense Forces Encyclopedia: The Paratroops*, in Hebrew (Tel Aviv: Revivim Publishing Co., 1981), 136-145; Bartov, *Dado: 48 Years and 20 Days*, 177-181; Wallach et al, *Carta's Atlas of Israel: The Third Decade, 1971-1981*, p. 40; *Special Ops Against Terrorism*, Defense Update International No. 85, p. 47; Milstein, *History of the Paratroops*, 1613-1637; Katz, *Follow Me! A History of Israel's Military Elite*, 112-116; Halevy and Livingstone, "The Killing of Abu Jihad," 160-164, 166, 168-172.

22. Sources used for constructing this account include: Dan, *The Finger of God*, 198-204; Kfir, *Israeli Defense Forces Encyclopedia*, 187-195; Wallach et al, *Carta's Atlas of Israel: The Third Decade, 1971-1981*, p. 115; Major (Res.) Louis Williams, "Entebbe Diary," *Israel Defense Forces Journal* (May 1985): 42-59; Avi Valentine, "Thunderball," in Hebrew, *Ha'aretz Weekly Supplement*, June 27, 1986, pp. 4-6, 10-11; Baruch Ran, "Entebbe: We Were There," in Hebrew, *Bamahane*, July 2, 1986, pp. 9-15, 41, 43-44; Miri Hanoch, "Motta Gur: How We Planned Operation Yonatan," in Hebrew, *Bita'on Heyl HaAvir*, July 1986, pp. 18-19; Lieutenant Colonel A., "Operation Yonatan: After the Gunfire," in Hebrew, no. 305, *Ma'arachot*, pp. 30-33.

3
Legitimizing International Terrorism: Is the Campaign Over?

Allan Gerson

The outward manifestations and images of terrorism—blood-stained floors, bullet-ridden victims, careening cars, masks, submachine guns, fire-bombed school buses, the remains of booby-trapped airliners—are all too familiar. We have seen these images throughout the 1980s. Perhaps the most poignant and the one that we can only picture in our imagination is the elderly American tourist, Leon Klinghoffer, being pushed in his wheelchair off the cruise ship *Achille Lauro* into the Mediterranean. Or perhaps it is that of the scattered remains of the victims of Pan Am 103 near Lockerbie, Scotland. No matter, as we enter the 1990s, we heave a collective sigh of relief as if terrorism were only something of the past.

Yes, the State Department still issues annual reports on state-sponsored terrorism. But the exercise seems increasingly a nuisance. Note, for example, the praise lavished by the White House in May 1990 on President Hafez al-Asad of Syria and the Iranian government for their cooperation in securing the release of two U.S. hostages in Lebanon. That very same day, a State Department report listed Iran and Syria as among the five nations that support terrorism.

Let us be clear. Under applicable U.S. law, Iran and Iraq are criminal co-conspirators in launching, aiding, and abetting terrorist acts. If this is generally recognized, although often ignored, the fact that international terrorists and their supporters seek to legitimize their activity seems widely misunderstood. This is the other face of international terrorism: manipulating international law to delegitimize the victim.

For more than two decades, the United Nations (UN) has been a hospitable arena for this kind of activity. A change has taken place, but whether it is temporary or permanent, illusory or substantial, is hard to know. What is certain is that the stand taken by the United States at the UN helped bring about this result. But victory is far from assured. The struggle against international terrorism remains that of Western values—particularly the rule of law—against its detractors. Without understanding the dynamics of that struggle, the past can prove to be prologue.

This study traces the development of the international effort to legitimate the select use of terrorism and the battle to counteract it. The 1970s witnessed the coming to fruition of a decade-long struggle to legitimate terrorism. The 1980s, beginning with President Ronald Reagan's first term of office, showed the beginning of a serious effort to take the battle to the other side and the changes in tactics forced upon pro-terrorist states. The 1990s involves the impact of the emerging post-Cold War order on terrorist movements.

Terrorism in the 1970s

The UN's involvement with international terrorism can be traced to 1972, when the murder of the Israeli athletes at the Munich Olympics stirred the General Assembly to place "the question of terrorism" on its agenda. That led to the establishment of a 35-member Ad Hoc Committee on International Terrorism. Soon, however, states that supported terrorism were able to work within the UN to turn that issue to their advantage. What began as an effort to condemn terrorism would become an exercise in its legitimation.

This was possible because the UN operates largely in blocs. In the 1970s, the radical Arab bloc, acting in concert with the Soviet bloc and much of the Non-Aligned Movement, lauded "national liberation movements" such as the PLO, the African National Congress (ANC), and the South West Africa People's Organization (SWAPO) as heralding a new age in which "colonial," "racist," or "alien" regimes would no longer exist. In that struggle for a more progressive community, all means, including terrorism, were deemed appropriate. Thus, detonating a bomb that killed schoolchildren was no longer a crime; it was a political act—providing, of course, that it was aimed at the overthrow of a racist, colonial, or alien regime. As a result, UN debates on terrorism in the early 1970s focused not on the victims of the Munich Olympics, but on the existing conditions that "forced" a resort to terrorism. The victims were to blame insofar as they stood in the way of the achievement of a new order.

By joining together in the General Assembly, the states supporting terrorism as an acceptable means of national liberation were able, in 1977, to ensure that the primary question put to the Ad Hoc Committee on International Terrorism became "the underlying causes" of terrorism.

Because the United States does not act as part of any bloc at the United Nations or in multilateral forums generally—having instead to rally support anew on each issue—the United States was unable to stop this move. The supporters of terrorism were too numerous and too powerful. In 1979, the Ad Hoc Committee issued its report, which was then adopted in full by the UN General Assembly. The report claimed to condemn all acts of international terrorism; in fact, it endorsed most of them. According to the report, "the continuation of repressive and terrorist acts committed by colonial, racist and alien regimes which denied peoples their legitimate right to self-determination and independence" were the key problems that led to terrorism. Thus, regimes deemed colonial, racist, or alien were determined to be the real terrorists.

In the mid- and late 1970s, the pro-terror forces scored several significant successes on other ideological fronts. The aim was to ensure that captured terrorists not be held as ordinary criminals, but treated as prisoners of war. Two years after the Munich massacres, a diplomatic conference was convened in Geneva on the revision of the 1949 Geneva Conventions. In 1977, the conference concluded its deliberation with the adoption of two new protocols.

Of these, the first was the more important. It provided that certain national liberation struggles were not to be considered internal civil strife. Under the rules of existing international law, other states could not intervene to end civil strife. They could intervene in civil war or in genuine international conflict. By deeming national liberation struggles to be international conflicts, the door was suddenly opened for foreign powers to freely assist insurgents seeking to subvert or overthrow existing governments. This proved a bonus for movements like SWAPO, the ANC, the Zambian resistance, the PLO, and others. State sponsorship of terrorism was legitimized overnight.

All would hinge on whether the insurgents were fighting "colonial," "racist," or "alien" regimes. If they were, they were entitled to outside intervention; if they were not, they could count on no outside support. Pro-Western regimes earned the approbation of being "colonial," "racist," or "alien." Thus, intervention by the Soviet Union, Cuba, Nicaragua, and other "progressive" regimes on behalf of insurgents was always permissible, while support for groups seeking to overthrow pro-socialist repressive regimes—like those in Nicaragua, Angola, or Afghanistan—was always impermissible.

Therefore, it is not surprising that the United States and every Western nation voted against adoption of Article 1 of the Protocol to the Geneva Convention when it was first proposed in 1974.[1] Yet, three years later when Article 1 came to a final vote, the United States and every other Western country changed their "no" votes of 1974 to abstentions.[2]

A similar thing happened in regard to adoption of Article 44 of Protocol I. Article 44 amends Article 4 of the Geneva Prisoner-of-War Convention, which accords the right of POW status to militiamen fulfilling the following conditions that would ensure that they could no longer be mistaken for civilians:

- that they wear a fixed distinctive sign (a uniform),
- they carry arms openly, and
- that they conduct operations in accordance with the laws and customs of war.

These provisions were based on the assumption that injury to innocent civilians would be reduced if steps were taken clearly to distinguish combatants from noncombatants. Formerly, militiamen seeking cover for military operations by disguising themselves as civilians would lose their rights to POW status and could be jailed as ordinary criminals. Article 44 of the new Protocol I accorded POW status to all militiamen regardless—or in spite of—their refusal to comply with any of the three conditions traditionally imposed by the laws of war on insurgents.

In 1974, the United States also voted against adoption of that article on the grounds that it would legitimate and encourage terrorism. In 1977, the United States changed that "no" vote to an abstention. So, too, did all the other Western nations, except Israel.

It is interesting to speculate—and it is relevant to contemporary events—why the United States abstained in 1977 on Articles 1 and 44 of Protocol I, after having so vociferously opposed their adoption in 1974. The record of the diplomatic conference is silent. Based on experience at the United Nations and multilateral forums, the answer is easy to surmise—the inability of U.S. diplomats to hold firm under pressure in multilateral negotiations. Because the United States is isolated, because it belongs to no bloc, and because U.S. diplomats are repeatedly told that their country's behavior is arrogant and stands in the path of the will of the "international community," the tendency is to tire and to begin to see grains of truth in the adversaries' allegations. It is easier to abstain on a controversial vote and remove oneself from involvement. But, of course, the opposite is true: An abstention signals capitulation.

Where incentives present themselves (the Protocols amended the Geneva Conventions in other ways, providing protection of medical personnel and the return of the remains of the fallen, which appealed to the military), the temptation to yield is even greater. There is another fact to be considered as well. The U.S. State Department bureaucracy, like those of most Western foreign offices, is international in outlook, enamored with consensus, and desirous of accommodation and the appearance of reasonableness and flexibility. Thus, as the 1970s came to a close, the combination of a relentless drive to legitimate terrorism and the tendency of U.S. diplomats to yield under sustained international pressure, succumbing to the temptation to go for an international agreement, whether intrinsically good or bad, produced the following results:

- It shifted the focus of international attention to the underlying causes and away from the victims.
- It changed the rules of engagement to permit foreign states to come to the aid of insurgent national liberation movements without viewing it as a violation of the principle of sovereign equality and nonintervention.
- It permitted captured terrorists to be treated as belligerents and not as ordinary criminals.

This was the situation that confronted the Reagan administration when it assumed power in the winter of 1980. The sobering demonstration of how the international community lined up on the issue of international terrorism soon followed. It left no room for doubt that the United States was alone in its position, isolated in a world in which acceptance of the Soviet/radical view of international law was increasingly gaining adherents.

Attention to this revelation occurred on Friday afternoon, May 14, 1979, at an Israeli lakeside resort town, Tiberias. A bomb set in a trash basket adjacent to a public garden exploded, killing 2 school children and maiming and wounding 36 others. Israeli authorities investigating the bombing traced it to a Palestinian living on the West Bank town of Ramallah. According to the confession of a captured accomplice, Abu Eain had set the time bomb, returned home as soon as the mission was accomplished, and then slipped across the Allenby bridge into Jordan.

Israeli authorities asked for the help of Interpol, the international police organization, in tracking down Abu Eain. Three months later, on August 17, 1979, Federal Bureau of Investigation (FBI) agents, acting on an Interpol warrant, located Abu Eain in Chicago and brought him before a local magistrates court seeking his extradition to Israel to stand trial for murder.

The matter seemed straightforward. A U.S.-Israeli treaty for mutual extradition of persons charged with criminal offenses had been in effect since 1963. It provided for extradition upon a demonstration that the requesting nation had obtained sufficient evidence to warrant an indictment. Here, Israel pointed to the signed confession by accomplices and to Abu Eain's efforts to elude apprehension. But Abu Eain's lawyers introduced a new element into the case, contending that even if Eain committed the acts with which he was charged, extradition should nevertheless be blocked because his actions were politically motivated. The political motivation: liberating his homeland, Palestine. Accordingly, his acts fell under the so-called "political offense" exception to a normally extraditable crime.

The U.S. Magistrate rejected the argument, finding sufficient evidence linking Abu Eain to the bombing. Political motives, ruled the Magistrate, did not excuse the killing of innocent civilians. On appeal, the Magistrate's decision was affirmed by the U.S. District Court in Chicago. Abu

Eain and his supporters then retained former U.S. Attorney-General Ramsey Clark to appeal that decision to the U.S. Court of Appeals for the Seventh Circuit.

On February 20, 1981, after hearing oral arguments, the three-member appeals' panel rendered its ruling. Affirming the District Court's order to extradite Abu Eain, Judge Harlington Wood, writing for the U.S. Court of Appeals, concluded that "the indiscriminate bombing of a civilian populace is not recognized as a protected political act" that would excuse the perpetrator of such an act from being subject to extradition to stand trial. To rule differently would mean that "nothing would prevent an influx of terrorists seeking safe haven in America. Those terrorists who flee to this country would avoid having to answer to anyone. The law is not so utterly absurd." That judgment was not to be shared by the community of nations at the United Nations.

After the U.S. Supreme Court turned down the petition by Abu Eain's lawyers that it review the Court of Appeals ruling, Abu Eain's supporters brought the matter to the United Nations. As the PLO representative stated at the time, what was at issue ranged far beyond the fate of one individual. It concerned the struggle waged at the United Nations to legitimate the use of "all available means" to "liberate" territory under "alien, racist, or colonial" rule—meaning, phrased differently, that Israeli civilians were legitimate targets. The proponents of this view were not about to let rulings of U.S. courts stand in their way. If necessary, they would show that the rulings of the U.S. courts stood in opposition to the overwhelming sentiment of the community of nations.

In the fall of 1981, the Abu Eain matter came up at the United Nations through the Economic and Social Council (ECOSOC), and then made its way to the General Assembly, eclipsing all the other issues that might have occupied the Assembly's attention at the time: the Iran-Iraq War, Pol Pot's massacres in Cambodia, guerrilla wars in Central America, the Soviet invasion of Afghanistan, fighting in Angola.

On April 28, 1981, several days after the U.S. Supreme Court had declined further review of Abu Eain's case, Jordan's Ambassador Hazim Nuseibeh requested that the General Assembly's Third Committee, dealing with social, humanitarian, and cultural affairs, take up the matter of Abu Eain under agenda item 91: "Torture and Other Cruel, Inhuman or Degrading Treatment of Punishment." The treatment

Nuseibeh was referring to was Abu Eain's supposed "torture" or other "cruel, inhuman, or degrading treatment" at the hands of the U.S. judicial system.

Although the U.S. Supreme Court had declined to reconsider the Court of Appeals affirmation of the decision to extradite Abu Eain, there was still one final tier of review available for opponents of extradition: under U.S. law, a finding by the secretary of state that extraordinary reasons of state dictated noncompliance with an other-- wise valid court order of extradition. William P. Clark, the deputy secretary of state and former California Supreme Court judge, under- took to review the matter. By this time, the future of Abu Eain had become an emotional touchstone throughout the Arab world. U.S. military installations, diplomatic posts, and U.S. embassy personnel were threatened with violence in the event Abu Eain were to be extradited to Israel.

On December 13, 1981, Clark made his decision, ruling that both policy and fidelity to law required the extradition to proceed; terrorism, regardless of motivation, could not be condoned: Threats directed against the United States could not be considered extraordinary foreign policy considerations for ignoring a court order.

Seven days after Clark's ruling, the United Nations acted. Seventy- five nations joined together to vote to condemn the U.S. legal system for ordering the extradition of Abu Eain. Only 21 nations voted against the resolution, and 73 nations chose to abstain, among them France, Spain, Turkey, Greece, Argentina, Brazil, Colombia, El Salvador, and the Philippines. The majority endorsed the use of "all available means"—here undeniably meaning terrorism—to combat "colonialism, racism, and alien rule"—here unmistakably meaning Israel. It was the apogee of the movement to legitimate terror.

The vote was a sobering lesson in the decline of U.S. influence and power at the United Nations and, more generally, in the decline of liberal values and liberal doctrines at the United Nations. The UN Charter was predicated on controlling the use of force. Now, an exception to an ostensibly universal prohibition on the use of unilater- al force (except in self-defense) was being carved out for national liberation movements that used terrorism as a principal means of struggle.

Terrorism in the 1980s

Four years later came another terrorist outrage. This one proved, however, too much to countenance even for those nations normally complacent about terrorism. The *Achille Lauro* set sail from Alexandria, Egypt, on the morning of Monday, October 7, 1985, after dropping off most of its 750 passengers for a bus tour of the Pyramids. A group of 97 remained on board the Italian cruise ship, most of them too old or infirm to climb the Pyramids. Four of the stay-behinds, however, were neither old nor infirm. Heavily armed terrorists seized the ship and threw the passengers on the floor of the dining room. During the following days, the *Achille Lauro* steamed around the Mediterranean as the terrorists issued demands for the freeing of 50 Palestinians being held in Israeli jails.[3]

The terrorists made two mistakes. The first was to commit an act of such barbarity—the assassination of a helpless, wheelchair-bound Leon Klinghoffer—that even the pro-terrorist states had to disassociate themselves from the open support of terrorism. The second was to believe that their friends in the Arab world were capable of protecting them from the United States. That mistake led to their capture over the Mediterranean by the U.S. Navy as they fled the scene of their crime on an EgyptAir passenger jet supplied by Egyptian President Hosni Mubarak.

In 1986, the United States again took a more determinedly military response toward terrorism, bombing several Libyan bases and nearly killing Libya's dictator, Mu'ammar Qadhafi, in reaction to his longtime support of terrorism in Europe and elsewhere and, most immediately, his support for the bombing of a discotheque in Berlin frequented by U.S. soldiers. The Libyan leader got the message, at least for a while, and Libyan support for terrorism decreased dramatically.[4] It was a clear signal that the United States was not prepared to tolerate states that openly supported terrorism. This, together with the international revulsion engendered by the *Achille Lauro* incident, would then lead to a switch in tactics by the pro-terrorist states as they sought to continue their support of terrorism under a new guise.

In the fall of 1985, following the *Achille Lauro* incident, Cuba introduced a draft resolution condemning as criminal all forms of terrorism while, at the same time, reaffirming in the preamble the legitimacy of liberation struggles against alien, colonial, and racist domination. Cuba, Libya, Syria, and others—with the help of the Soviet Union—opted to coopt the language of anti-terrorism and thereby sow confusion by making the states principally supporting terrorism the prime movers of a UN resolution to condemn it as criminal.

The United States, again eager for consensus and believing that the articulation of antiterrorist sentiment, no matter how generally defined and under whose sponsorship, was a positive accomplishment in itself, decided to support the resolution. The other Western states followed suit, and the passage of the Cuban-Syrian sponsored resolution was hailed by the United States as a turning point in the war against terrorism. UN Secretary-General Javier Perez de Cuellar proclaimed that it represented "a truly important achievement...a major move, on the widest possible scale, to deal with a problem having universal implications."

By the terms of that Cuban-Syrian antiterrorism resolution, states were called upon to submit their views on concrete measures to implement the resolution's antiterrorism consensus. The true face of the sponsors soon became transparent as the 1987 session of the General Assembly debated implementation of that resolution. Syria, the first to respond, proposed the convening of an international conference to study terrorism so that steps might be taken to differentiate properly between terrorism, which was now illegitimate, and terrorism that should not be called terrorism. Syria's communiqué to the UN Secretary-General, quoting President Hafez al-Asad, spoke of an absence "of definite agreed international criteria that would enable the international community to distinguish clearly between terrorism, which must be condemned and combatted, and national struggle, which must be protected and supported." Therefore, it called for "the establishment of an international commission to define terrorism and to lay down the demarcation line separating it from the struggle of peoples for their just causes and the liberation of their territories."[5]

Egypt was the next to respond. Demonstrating again the intimidating effect of UN bloc politics on moderate states, Egypt, eager to regain prominence in the Arab world even at the expense of maintaining good relations with the West and peace with Israel, joined the effort.

The Soviets supported Syria's proposal. The United States, speaking through one of its public delegates, Representative George Crockett, stated that Syria's proposed conference was not a useful way to deal with the problem because it "would inevitably maximize international disagreement." Because British intelligence had directly linked Syria to a recent attempted bombing at Heathrow Airport, the European Economic Community weighed in against the conference idea, this time in much stronger terms than their U.S. counterparts, calling for the isolation of Syria through a series of diplomatic and economic measures.[6]

Syria and its backers did not, however, succeed because their proposal failed to command enough international support. In a face-saving gesture, Syria was compelled to tone down the proposal so that it merely reaffirmed the previous UN condemnations of terrorism in all forms and invited further discussion of the means of combating it.[7] It was a setback for Syria and the states supporting the drive to legitimate certain kinds of terrorism, thanks to a unified stand by Western nations.

Terrorism in the 1990s

The PLO had long been identified by the Reagan administration as the hub of the wheel of international terrorism. In December 1988, the PLO was ready to assume a new image, and the U.S. administration was only too eager to help. PLO Chairman Yassir Arafat made a series of statements that lent themselves to the interpretation—if one were not inclined to examine contradictory statements—that he would recognize Israel, accept UN Resolutions 242 and 338, and renounce terrorism. As the Reagan administration neared the end of its term, a new era of U.S.-Soviet cooperation seemed to be burgeoning. The urge for a quick diplomatic success in the Middle East, as well as elsewhere, gave extra impetus for jumping at the statements made by the PLO (some of which were formulated in Washington) as signs of a major breakthrough. Within days, the United States opened, for the first time, direct contacts with the PLO. The United States thus committed itself to trying to coopt the PLO by assuming, despite the lack of evidence, that it had in fact renounced terrorism. The PLO would be challenged to live up to that renunciation.

At the time of this "breakthrough," the U.S. government announced that it would hold Arafat responsible for any acts of terror by the PLO and its many member groups. Although Arafat himself and his immediate high command appear to have largely kept that promise, several groups within the PLO openly claimed responsibility for new terrorist attacks against Israel. Arafat has said that these groups, such as the Popular Front for the Liberation of Palestine, the Palestine Liberation Front, and the Democratic Front for the Liberation of Palestine (DFLP), are outside his control. The U.S. State Department concurred.[8] But the June 1990 foiled sea attack against Israeli civilian targets on the Tel Aviv coastline changed that. The extensive links at every level between Arafat and these groups, all represented on the PLO's Executive Committee, made his denials of knowledge of their activities difficult to accept. The U.S. promise to hold Arafat responsible for PLO actions finally had to be enforced, and the U.S.-PLO "dialogue" was suspended when Arafat refused to even so much as reprimand those responsible for the planned attack.

As we look to the future in a post-Cold War era, how does the new set of international relations affect the battle against terrorism? Obviously, insofar as the Soviet Union and its Eastern bloc partners have formally announced an end to the training of terrorist groups—and no longer push the ideology legitimating terrorist and national liberation groups—the West has reaped a major victory. Insofar as the Soviet Union now appears willing to commit itself to the rule of law as a governing principle of international relations, a major success has been scored. After all, the designation "terrorism" rests on the abnegation of the concept of a single standard that underlies the idea of the rule of law. International terrorism appears increasingly at the end of its tether. Not only has international support for terrorism declined in terms of training and support, which it has received for decades from the Soviets and Non-Aligned Movement, but the ideological foundations for support of terrorism appear to have been shaken.

Whether the Soviet Union has abandoned its ideological commitment to support national liberation struggles remains uncertain. Like all organized subversion, terrorism flourishes on the degree of moral support and approval that it receives. It will continue to seek that support from states who most benefit by terrorism. The collapse of the dual pillars of communism—expansion abroad and repression at home—will not curb the actions of states like Iraq, Syria, Libya, and Iran that benefit from terrorist activity. Each of these states appears ready to continue involvement in terrorist activities with or without Soviet support.

It would be a mistake to believe that these remaining vestiges of international terrorism can be accommodated under the rule of law. Their sponsors have no allegiance to the concept of universal standards. They seem likely to continue to try to market their deadly wares, although at considerably greater risk and with less encouragement and support of an international community than in the 1970s and early 1980s. In the new post-Cold War order—no differently than orders that prevailed in other periods of international stability—it is the power of deterrence that will prove determinative in curbing the resort to the unlawful use of force.

Notes

1. The March 1974 vote in committee on that paragraph was 70 votes in favor and 21 against.

2. The vote was 87 in favor with only 1 against—Israel—and 11 abstentions.

3. See David C. Martin and John Walker, *Best Laid Plans: The Inside Story of America's War Against Terrorism* (New York: Simon and Schuster), chapter 9.

4. Ibid., chapter 10.

5. Communiqué from the Government of Syria to the UN Secretary-General, December 19, 1986.

6. Communiqué from the European Economic Community to the UN Secretary-General, March 31, 1987.

7. See Paul Lewis, "Syria, Isolated at UN, Drops Terrorism Plan," *The New York Times*, December 2, 1987.

8. "PLO Terrorism 1989-1990: Violating the Terms of the U.S.-PLO Dialogue," Anti-Defamation League of the B'nai B'rith, March 1990.

4
Airline Safety: The Price of Security

William M. Carley

W hen Pan Am Flight 103 was brought down over Scotland by a terrorist bomb a few days before Christmas 1988, the event prompted a closer scrutiny of airport and airline defenses against bombs. It also prompted a reevaluation of the way government—and particularly U.S. government agencies—aid and regulate the security aspects of airline operations. Examination of these issues inevitably has involved the interplay between private, profit-making airlines and the interests of governments in preventing terrorist acts.

The result of this scrutiny has not been reassuring. Because of the nature and location of the threat, as well as the structure, functions, and personnel involved in countering the threat, it has become clear that there is no substantially effective deterrent in place. Moreover, there is a real question as to whether an effective deterrent can be developed, barring some breakthrough in technology to develop a small, fast, and cost-effective device that can detect a bomb under all circumstances.

Thus, airlines and governments that are targets of terrorism find themselves in an extraordinarily difficult position. They face a deadly threat—that can have enormous political repercussions—for which there is no answer. Unlike the U.S. measures that succeeded in stopping Cubans from hijacking U.S. carriers to Havana in the 1970s, there are no fully effective measures to prevent terrorists from placing bombs aboard aircraft.

Success breeds imitation. The spectacular success of Middle East terrorists against the Pan Am Flight 103 was quickly copied. Terrorists put a bomb aboard a UTA French airliner flying from Chad to Paris in September 1989, which killed 171. Terrorists in Colombia, apparently drug cartel members, placed a bomb aboard an Avianca plane in November 1989, which killed all 107 on board.

The Colombian example amply demonstrates the potential political impact of terrorist activities. The Avianca plane was on a Bogata-Cali run, a business route that is the rough equivalent of the shuttle between New York and Washington. "It was as if someone had bombed the shuttle and, as you might expect, the Avianca disaster killed some of the cream of Colombia's business leadership," says Michael Ackerman, a former CIA employee who has specialized in Latin American affairs. There is little doubt that the Avianca bombing, along with a wave of bombings on the ground, has played a role in the recent shift of Colombian public opinion toward some sort of "accommodation" with the drug cartels in an effort to halt the violence. In sum, the Avianca bombing turned out to be quite successful in political terms, from the terrorists' point of view.

The threat of aircraft bombings is growing. Some analysts even believe that the bombing of Pan Am 103 has understated the real intentions of the terrorists, who had constructed four other bombs with barometric triggers, all obviously aimed at aircraft. But for the fact that West German police arrested some members of the gang and eventually found the other bombs, several other planes might have been knocked out of the sky.

To understand how airlines and governments have come into this difficult and dangerous position, the structure and functioning of the aviation security apparatus must be reviewed. For the most part, this analysis will focus on the U.S. security apparatus, which has the greatest influence on U.S. carriers.

The Federal Aviation Administration

As a bureaucracy, the Federal Aviation Administration (FAA) is not particularly suited to setting up or overseeing any security apparatus. The predecessor of the agency was created in the 1920s, with the purpose of installing a system of airports, radio communications, and the like that would foster the development of the airline industry. Another goal was to license—and in some cases ground—barnstorming private pilots who were killing themselves and others at a fairly rapid rate. Throughout the years, the agency has handled other duties, such as certifying as airworthy new aircraft that companies (such as Boeing) might propose to build. After two airliners—TWA and United—collided over the Grand Canyon in 1956, killing everyone on both planes, the agency got deeply involved in the business of guiding aircraft along defined routes.

As airline traffic boomed during the past 20 years, the air traffic control function has come to dominate the FAA bureaucracy. Of the 48,000 FAA personnel now employed, about 25,000 are assigned to air traffic control functions. This means that the top leadership of the agency generally comes from air controller ranks. (Even the former head of the FAA security department was at one time a controller.)

In contrast to the tens of thousands in air traffic control, the FAA security department now numbers slightly more than 500, and that reflects a major increase since the 1985 TWA hijacking in Beirut. Thus, the security function is relatively insignificant in the overall FAA mission.

As it turns out, the FAA security department is not designed to do much. As the agency itself notes, the FAA is supposed to provide "leadership" in identifying the threat, prescribing security requirements, providing technical assistance, and enforcing regulations. It is the airlines, however, that are to do the pick-and-shovel work. According to the FAA, it is the duty of the airlines to maintain security programs, screen passengers and carryon items, secure checked baggage, and protect aircraft.

Some believe the security structure was designed this way in part to minimize the cost of security to the federal government and in part to minimize the federal government's legal liability when an airliner is hijacked or bombed.[1]

Whatever the motives in setting up this system, it has resulted in a splintering of responsibility for security functions. The FAA identifies the threat, makes and enforces the rules; the airlines are supposed to do the work. Responsibility is split even more because not just one airline, but nearly a dozen major U.S. carriers must each operate security systems. And at each airline, the security operation is very much the stepchild of the carrier's overall operations.

Just what are the FAA and airlines up against? To understand the nature of the threat, it is worth considering the case of Mohammad Rashid.

The Traveling Terrorist

On August 11, 1982, an attractive couple and their young child appeared to be on vacation, flying from Hong Kong to Tokyo aboard Pan Am. In fact, however, the man was a terrorist who was quietly and unobtrusively slipping a tiny, powerful bomb beneath his seat cushion before he and his family got off in Tokyo. On the plane's next flight, as the Pan Am jet neared Honolulu, the bomb exploded. The blast tore the legs off a Japanese teenager who happened to be in that seat, and he bled to death. Fifteen other passengers were injured.

The event announced the arrival of some new actors and increasingly sophisticated bombs onto the stage of international terrorism. The man who placed the bomb beneath the seat allegedly was Mohammad Rashid, a member of several Palestinian terrorist groups, which have since placed bombs in planes around the world. Rashid is also suspected of involvement in the bombing of a TWA jet as it approached Athens in 1986, killing four.

Arrested in Greece in 1988, Rashid has been in an Athens jail ever since. He denied involvement in the bombing and was scheduled to be tried in Athens in 1991. He successfully fought extradition to the United States where he had been indicted for the murder, assault, and aircraft sabotage of the Pan Am bombing. The federal district court indictment against him in Washington, as well as information from other sources, provides a detailed account of his groups' alleged exploits.

The story begins with a group called the Arab Organization of 15 May, a group opposed to the existence of Israel. The 15 May group aimed not only at Israeli targets, but also at U.S. targets because of its huge financial and military support of Israel. The brains behind 15 May is a Palestinian, Husayn al-Umari (also known as Abu Ibrahim), who made his headquarters in Baghdad, Iraq. Ibrahim, as it turned out, was to become rather expert in bomb building.

One of Ibrahim's right-hand men was Rashid, a tall, slender Palestinian who is now about 40 years old. Another important figure was Rashid's Austrian wife, Christine Pinter. "The couple," according to a U.S. State Department memo, "supposedly had been trained by Abu Ibrahim at his headquarters in Baghdad and were allegedly given five bombs" to place on airplanes.

On July 15, 1982, according to the indictment in Washington, Rashid submitted a visa application—including a photograph—to the Japanese embassy in Baghdad. He used a false name, Mohammad Harouk, on his application. He also submitted visa applications for his wife and child, using false names for them, too. Three visas to enter Japan were issued that same day.

A few weeks later, the Rashids made their way to Singapore. There, Rashid bought Pan Am tickets for the three to Tokyo via Hong Kong, where they stopped over for two days. On August 11, the three boarded a Pan Am jumbo jet in Hong Kong for the last leg of their trip.

Sitting together in row 47, the Rashids were noticed by a flight attendant who thought they were "a nice family," according to a former Pan Am executive. During the trip, Rashid allegedly slipped the bomb under seat 47K, a window seat. The three left the plane in Tokyo and disappeared into the crowds.

After the bombed jet made it to Honolulu airport and the bloodied and frightened passengers stumbled out, FBI agents began an inquiry. Clues were few. "Right now, we're totally in the dark," an FBI official in Honolulu said at the time.

But two weeks later and half a world away, one clue did emerge. While a woman was cleaning a Pan Am jet in Rio de Janeiro, she looked under seat cushions, apparently hoping to find loose change. But when she pulled up one of the seats, a maroon vinyl packet the size of a small book fell to the floor. The cleaning woman informed her supervisor; he called police.

The next day in Washington, a small Federal Aviation Administration jet took off, carrying FAA and FBI officials. They flew to Rio and brought the disarmed bomb back to Washington. In FBI labs, chemical analysis compared the explosive used in the Honolulu bomb with the explosive in the Rio packet. They were identical. The Rio bomb, because it was intact, gave U.S. officials their first good look at what they were up against.

"It was frightening," says a U.S. official. "It was obviously designed to beat the [security] system—and it did." For one thing, the electronic components used to time and trigger the bomb were miniaturized, about the size of a digital watch, making them very nearly undetectable. For another, the Rio bomb contained about three-fourths of a pound of plastic explosive, which cannot be detected readily on most x-ray machines, thus frustrating airport security checkpoints.

And instead of a single trigger (typically a simple timing device), the bomb contained a double mechanism—a timer that was activated only when a passenger was sitting on the seat cushion. That, says the U.S. official, maximizes the chance that someone will be in the seat when the bomb explodes.

FBI agents in Honolulu and other cities, meanwhile, were interviewing Pan Am flight attendants, checking Pan Am tickets and passengers' visa records to reconstruct the itinerary of the occupant of seat 47K just before the Tokyo-Honolulu hop. They tracked Harouk and his family back from Tokyo to Hong Kong to Singapore and, ultimately, to Baghdad. There, in Baghdad, they found the pictures submitted to the Japanese embassy with the visa applications.

The true occupant of 47K—Mohammad Rashid—had a prior criminal record. He had been jailed on drug charges in Greece from 1972 to 1977. He was jailed in Turkey in 1978 for selling a stolen car, but escaped the next year. He was arrested in Milan in 1980 on suspicion of drug smuggling and was then expelled from the country. Because of the arrests, security officials in several nations had good photos of Rashid. "We took the picture of 'Harouk' and found he was really Rashid," an FBI official says.

Even while U.S. investigators were making progress, however, the 15 May group tried to strike again. In December 1983, a British woman living in Athens flew to Tel Aviv to buy religious artifacts, flew to London to sell them, and then returned to Athens. She was unaware that her business associate in Athens, a Jordanian named Fuad Hussain Shara, had apparently given her a suitcase to carry merchandise that also concealed a bomb. The bomb had been set to explode on her El Al Israel flight to or from Tel Aviv, but it failed to detonate.

CIA agents in Greece somehow heard about and obtained the suitcase. In their examination, U.S. bomb experts concluded that the device had the earmarks of an Abu Ibrahim bomb. In this bomb, however, the 15 May leader had developed another type of trigger. A barometric device was built in to sense the drop in atmospheric pressure as the plane rose into the sky. The barometer activated the timer on the bomb, so that it would explode in flight. The timer could also be set to detonate the bomb after the plane had made several takeoffs and landings. By then, the bomber could be safely on the ground and making his getaway.

This bomb had another advantage. It could be placed in a checked suitcase. Checked luggage gets much less scrutiny from airport security people than do carryon bags. (The suitcase used by the British woman had made it through security in Athens, Tel Aviv, and London. The latter two locations supposedly have some of the best security in the world.) A bomb in a checked bag has another advantage; compared to a small carryon bag, a bomb in a checked bag can be much larger.

To detect bombs set off by changes in barometric pressure, several major airports around the world—including London Heathrow and Tel Aviv—have installed special pressure chambers. Suspicious bags can be placed in the chambers, which mimic the drop in pressure that occurs when a plane ascends. But the chambers have only limited effectiveness. In the electronics now used to trigger bombs, a timer can run as long as months before setting off an explosion. Airport security officials, hoping not to delay legitimate luggage any longer than necessary, usually do not leave bags in pressure chambers more than a few hours. Beyond that, there is the problem of which bag among tens of thousands going through major airports every day is suspicious enough to place in a chamber.

The British woman who unwittingly took her Abu Ibrahim bomb to Tel Aviv, London, and back to Athens may, directly or indirectly, have been duped by Rashid, as well as her Jordanian business associate. Rashid has spent a lot of time in Athens. He has been charged with using Abu Ibrahim's bombs. The indictment against Rashid alleges he "would recruit and help to recruit persons to wittingly and unwittingly transport explosives."

About 1984, according to a State Department fact sheet, the 15 May group appeared to disband, but most of its operatives moved into a similar anti-Israeli, anti-American group run by a Palestinian who calls himself "Colonel Hawari." Among those switching from 15 May to the Hawari group, State Department officials say, were Rashid and a woman using the name May Mansur. Rashid acted as the "control" of Mansur, the U.S. officials say.

On the morning of April 2, 1986, Mansur presented herself at a TWA ticket counter in Cairo saying she wished to fly to Athens to transact business and then to Lebanon, where she said she ran a dress boutique in Tripoli. According to a former executive of the airline, TWA officials in Cairo were suspicious because she had no visa to enter Greece. In response to questions, she explained that she was going to transact her business in the Athens airport transit lounge, where she would not need a visa. She was allowed to board.

She sat in seat 10F of the Boeing 727 on which she flew to Athens and there got off. The TWA jet continued on to Rome, then headed back for Athens. En route, a bomb exploded under seat 10F, ripping a hole in the fuselage. Four passengers were sucked out of the plane at 15,000 feet.

FBI experts again compared the plastic explosive used on the TWA plane to those used on the Pan Am jets and found them to be identical. But the bombers may have improved their technique. U.S. authorities speculate that Mansur smuggled the bomb on board in pieces. A tiny electronic timer, for example, might have been concealed in the cassette player she carried, the plastic explosive in other hand luggage. When Mansur went to the lavatory on the plane, she could have snapped the components together to assemble a working bomb.[2]

The bomb was improved another way. The devices aboard the Pan Am planes in 1982 were 75 percent explosive in a latex binder. The TWA bomb in 1986 had been increased to nearly 85 percent explosive. "That means significantly more punch in the same size bomb," says Billie Vincent, a former FAA security director.

Meanwhile, Rashid, tracked by U.S. intelligence agencies for years, finally showed up at the Athens airport on a flight on May 30, 1988. Tipped by the United States, Greek police were there to arrest him.

In the initial investigation of the 1982 Pan Am bombing near Honolulu, FBI agents had sought to build a case against whoever was responsible. They looked for fingerprints of Mohammad Harouk around his seat, on his Pan Am ticket, and on travel papers. They finally found prints on his ticket. And the prints matched those of Rashid taken when he was jailed by Greek authorities in the 1970s.

After reviewing the evidence, Greek courts approved Rashid's extradition to the United States. But the Greek prime minister must give the final approval, and, thus far, Rashid still has not been extradited to the United States.

The Airline Response

As is evident from the Rashid case, the terrorist threat to U.S. carriers spans the globe. Rashid left his tracks in Istanbul, Athens, Milan, Baghdad, Singapore, Hong Kong, and Tokyo. There is evidence of Abu Ibrahim's bombs passing through airports in Hong Kong, Tokyo, Rio de Janiero, Tel

Aviv, London, Cairo, Athens, and Rome (all undetected except for the cleaning lady's chance find in Rio).

As is also evident from the Rashid case, it is not easy to catch the terrorists and bring them to trial. Nearly six years elapsed between Rashid's fateful 1982 flight to Tokyo and his 1988 arrest in Greece. Two more years have elapsed, and he still has not been extradited for trial in the United States. "We've been very successful in identifying terrorist bombers rather quickly," says Floyd I. Clarke, an FBI official who has served as director of criminal investigations for the bureau. But, he adds, "We've been less successful and slower in bringing these people to justice."

Moreover, Rashid is one of the few terrorist bombers to have been apprehended. Even if several were to be caught, there is a ready supply of young terrorists in Lebanon and elsewhere, already trained by the various factions.

As a result of these factors, the terrorist threat is not going to go away. It is also clear that the main threat to U.S. carriers is not in the United States, but overseas. The U.S. airlines, as a result, must mount their defense against future terrorist bombs in airports around the world.

There is still another lesson to be drawn from the Rashid case. The airline response to the bombers must address the increasingly sophisticated and hard-to-detect explosives. One would hope, therefore, that airline screening of both carryon and checked bags would become more sophisticated.

Because of the structure of the U.S. security system, that has not yet happened. As noted earlier, the FAA's main role has been to issue rules and enforce them, leaving the burden of financing and operating the security system to the individual carriers. But in the past decade of airline deregulation, a once-sedate business has turned into cutthroat competition. Major carriers, ranging from Braniff International to People's Express, have gone into bankruptcy or have been forced to sell out to a stronger competitor.

Because of this atmosphere, airline executives have come under intense pressure to cut costs. One of their expenses, sometimes as much as 40 percent of operating costs, is personnel. Hence, airline executives have tried hard to cut wage and benefits costs.

When it comes to security, the carriers have generally opted to contract the work out to private security firms. The work is generally awarded to the security firm making the lowest bid. Unconstrained by the high levels of airline wages negotiated by powerful airline unions, these private security firms are able to provide low-cost labor.

There is another factor. These contracted security personnel—not being airline employees—are not eligible for the free flight benefits granted by virtually every airline to its own employees. Low wages and lack of benefits mean a low-skilled work force, troubled by high turnover rates. (At some carriers, the yearly turnover among screeners is said to approach 50 percent.) Coupled with this problem is a security system that depends heavily on the skill of the operator for effective detection.

In addition, the security systems currently in place were set up not to detect bombs, but pistols and knives carried by hijackers (Cubans in the early 1970s, Arabs later on). To detect guns and knives, the systems depend on x-ray machines for carryon bags and on metal detectors that passengers walk through.

Old-fashioned metal timers and wiring for bombs were detectable by x-rays, but as was evident in the Rashid case, terrorists are now using miniaturized components for timers. And these timers are being disguised, as in wiring, as parts of radios or cassette players. For the explosives, the terrorists are using the hard-to-detect plastic explosives.

"We've been trying to force the x-ray machines into a bomb-detector role, and they're just not designed for that," says a former airline security director.

Recently, enhanced x-ray machines have begun reaching the market. These machines can distinguish low-atomic-weight organic materials— that, among many other things include plastic and other explosives—and can assign a specific color to them on a TV screen, thus indicating that the operator should take a closer look. But all x-ray machines, new or old, depend on interpretations by operators. A 1987 Transporation Department task force took a close look at the operators. With wages low, sometimes barely above the minimum wage, it was hard to recruit good people, the task force found. Two contractors interviewed by the task force said fast-food chains were their chief competitors for staff. "The restaurants occasionally paid more...and even if pay were the same, had the advantage because they provide meals as well," the task force said.

With pressure on to hold costs down, not much money has been devoted to training. The task force described training of U.S. x-ray screeners as "perfunctory."

Perhaps the biggest problem, however, is the nature of the job itself. "Anyone standing in front of a monitor watching suitcase after suitcase go by is bound over time to become tired and inattentive," the task force reported. At peak periods, it added, screeners are confronted with "long lines of anxious passengers, putting the screening crew under extreme pressure" to rush bags through.

In Europe, government employees usually screen passengers, with U.S. carriers often performing a second screening. But the same problems afflict screeners overseas.

Checked bags are an even bigger problem than carryon items. Because Pan Am 103 was destroyed by a bomb apparently placed aboard a Pan Am jet in Frankfurt, the FAA has required U.S. carriers to x-ray or search all checked bags in Europe and the Mideast. But the carriers must handle a huge volume of checked bags at peak periods. At Frankfurt, for example, Pan Am alone must load more than 4,000 bags in four hours. That means searching all the bags is impossible, and x-raying them all with care is very difficult.

Some security experts believe that the FAA order on checked bags, which applies only to Europe and the Middle East, is creating a Maginot Line and that terrorists in the future will just attempt to evade this defense. Security experts note that screeners at airports in Africa or Latin America are likely to be poorly paid, unskilled, and easily bribed to look the other way. As it is, bags now checked in these areas normally are neither searched nor x-rayed anyway. They are put, unexamined, on airplanes.

The FAA also has issued regulations requiring U.S. carriers to install thermo-neutron activation (TNA) devices at major U.S. and foreign terminals. These are the first machines that can specifically detect plastic explosives. The machines fire neutrons at checked bags riding on a conveyor belt; the neutrons cause each element in a bag to emit gamma rays in a distinctive signature, and computer analysis of the rays can pick out plastic explosives. The machines supposedly operate with 95 percent accuracy, but some experts maintain that plastic explosives configured in a certain way will not be detected.

There are other problems with TNA devices. The machines are big. The first TNA unit installed at TWA's terminal at Kennedy Airport in New York required construction of a new building. In addition, the machines use radioactive devices to operate. This has made some foreign nations quite reluctant to allow the machines in their airports. The machines also are costly, about $1 million each currently. With production of the machines just now gearing up, it will be several years, at the earliest, before these machines will be working in adequate numbers at major airports.

To reduce the checked-bag threat, airlines now are supposed to match each bag checked with a passenger on board, making anyone knowingly checking a bag with a bomb a potential suicide. Terrorists have countered by using unwitting bomb carriers. The British woman who flew Athens-Tel Aviv-London-Athens, unwittingly carrying a bomb that failed to detonate, is a case in point. Another example was a young Irish woman who passed through London Heathrow security—including an x-ray machine—in 1986 with a suitcase containing a bomb prepared by her Arab boyfriend. The timer was concealed in a calculator, the bomb in the bottom of the suitcase. El Al security men at the gate discovered the bomb just before the woman boarded. Of course, it is not always the case that bombs fail to detonate or are found just before boarding. Investigators believe the bomb that destroyed Pan Am 103 was checked by an unwitting traveler at Frankfurt.

The Air India case is a classic example of how all these problems—airport workers trying to check hordes of passengers quickly, poorly trained security screeners, and loopholes in the system—can come together to produce disaster.

The Bombing of Air India

According to Royal Canadian Mounted Police documents and investigations by Canadian and Indian aviation officials, Air India was worried about its Canadian operations in 1985. Toronto and Vancouver have sizable Sikh populations, and June 1985 was the first anniversary of the storming of the Sikh Golden Temple in Amritsar, India, by Indian troops. Sikh retaliation seemed possible.

Early in 1985, Air India became the first and only airline in Canada to acquire x-ray machines to scan checked bags. It also asked Canadian authorities for greater police protection, including bomb-sniffing dogs. Air India had only a once-a-week flight to Canada that landed in Toronto, doubled back to Montreal, and then returned to New Delhi via London.

In Toronto, the Mounted Police provided four extra police for the flight—one in a car parked under the plane's right wing, another in a car patrolling the apron, one at Air India's check-in counter, and a fourth at the boarding gate. Similar protection was provided in Montreal. However, the authorities declined to provide any dogs to sniff out bombs.

A few days before the June 22, 1985, Air India flight, a man with an Indian accent phoned a Canadian Pacific (CP) Airlines agent. He wanted reservations for two men. The first was to travel on CP Air from Vancouver to Tokyo and then transfer to Air India for a flight to Bangkok.

"I went back to him and suggested that he should take a carrier [to Bangkok] other than Air India" because of better connections and a lower fare, the CP Air agent later told Mounted Police according to a transcript of the interview. "Then he said it was all right; he didn't mind what the fare was. So then, I quoted him a fare, and he said it was all right, which is most unusual with Indians because they always have to have the lowest fare."

The reservation for the second traveler was for a flight from Vancouver to Toronto, connecting with the Air India flight heading for Montreal, London, and New Delhi. The reservation for the Air India leg was standby, not confirmed.

The next day, an Indian man appeared at a CP Air office in Vancouver and paid more than $3,000 in cash for the tickets. Saturday morning, June 22, was busy at Vancouver airport, with long lines at check-in counters. A CP Air agent later told the Mounted Police that when an Indian man named Mr. Singh reached the head of her line, "He wanted his bag checked to Delhi. And I said, 'I can't do that sir, because you're not confirmed on the [Air India] flight.'" As a security measure, CP Air forbade checking bags for standby passengers.

While travelers in line fretted, an argument ensued. "He said, 'But I phoned Air India, and I am confirmed on the flight.'" She said she responded that he "might have been confirmed in their computer but not confirmed in our computer."

Singh continued to insist, arguing that he would have to go to the trouble of transferring his bag at Toronto if it was not checked all the way to New Delhi. The CP Air agent continued to decline. "And [then] he said, 'Wait, I'll go get my brother for you,'" she recalled. "And the lineups were so busy, I thought you gotta be crazy. And I said to him, 'I don't have time to talk to your brother'....So, he came back, and I said, 'OK, I'll check it through.'"

Shortly afterward, a person also using the name Singh checked a bag at Vancouver for the flight to Tokyo connecting on Air India to Bangkok. The two Singhs did not board their planes, CP Air records show. CP Air had failed to match checked bags with passengers on board.

When the CP Air jet arrived in Toronto, airport workers transferred bags to other carriers, including Air India. Air India had contracted with Burns International Security Systems for baggage screening and other security. On June 22, Naseem Nanji, a Burns employee, was working only her second shift on the x-ray machine. "I was told to look for guns," she later told the Mounted Police. "I didn't receive any instructions on how to look for a bomb; I was told to look for funny wiring or connections." She did not find any bombs.

Then the x-ray machine broke down, or as Jim Post, another Burns worker put it, "everything went blank" on the screen. So, Post picked up a hand-held "sniffer," which detects some explosives, and began screening bags with that. He found nothing. Asked by Mounted Police whether he had taken the passenger-screening course required by the Canadian government, Post replied: "No, I was taken out and dumped in and told to do the job of checking the baggage." Even if well trained, he might not have found the bomb anyway because sniffers do not detect plastic explosives at all, and some units do a poor job anyway.

Although Singh's bag went on board Air India, he did not, records show. Like CP Air, Air India did not match bags and passengers. The Air India jumbo jet took off, stopped briefly in Montreal, then took off again for London. Hours later and 110 miles west of Ireland, it blew up, killing the 329 persons on board. One hour earlier, a bag that had arrived in Tokyo on the CP Air flight from Vancouver had exploded in a baggage cart while on its way to an Air India jet. That bomb killed two Japanese airport workers.

Police have been hunting for the Air India bombers. Later in 1985, Mounted Police arrested Inderjit Singh Reyat, a Sikh electrician living near Vancouver, partly because he was linked to another Sikh militant also living in the area. Lacking hard evidence, the Mounted Police released Reyat, who then moved to Britain.

Despite extensive salvage efforts, bomb fragments could not be obtained from the jet that exploded over the Atlantic. But in Japan, police meticulously examined every bit of debris from the baggage-cart bomb. They found more than 100 bits and pieces that they believe were used in the bomb: 92 pieces of a Sanyo radio model FMT 611K, which concealed the bomb; 15 of a car clock timer; 13 of an Eveready battery; pieces of an electrical switch; and traces of "Liquid Fire" starting fluid, gunpowder, a high-explosive charge, and a blasting cap, as well as some green adhesive tape.

In a search of Reyat's home in Canada, Mounted Police found a receipt for a Sanyo radio, also model FMT 611K. According to the Canadian government legal counsel in London who was seeking Reyat's extradition to Canada, Reyat had bought the Sanyo radio in a local Woolworth store six weeks before the Air India disaster. The counsel also said in the extradition proceeding that Mounted Police also discovered that Reyat had bought a car clock timer and an electrical switch at a Radio Shack store. And at his home, the Mounted Police found green adhesive tape matching that found by Japanese investigators.

In February 1988, while on his way to work at the Jaguar PLC plant in Coventry, Reyat encountered a police roadblock. Special antiterrorist police were on hand. Reyat was arrested on Canadian charges that he built the bomb that killed the two Japanese airport workers.

The bombing of Air India had a traumatic effect on Canadian government officials. They launched an enormous effort to upgrade security, ordering higher pay and better training for screeners, a system to match bags with passengers on board, and x-raying of checked bags when threats warrant. Canadian security now is much tighter. One example is that the metal detectors passengers must walk through are tuned to pick up the slightest trace of metal—in one case, sounding an alarm when a passenger with just two pennies in his pocket passed through it at the Toronto airport. (In contrast, passengers can walk through the loosely tuned metal detectors in the United States with much heavier metal objects and still avoid tripping an alarm.)

Pan Am's Security

The Air India bombing in 1985 presumably taught airlines around the world some lessons: Make sure every bag is matched by a passenger on board. Make sure airline security screeners are well trained, using the proper equipment and proper procedures. More than three years later, some carriers—including Pan Am—did not appear to have learned these lessons.

To understand the reasons requires a glance at Pan Am history. In 1984—there was a battle in Pan Am's executive suite. The winners were Martin Shugrue and Gerald Gitner, who became vice chairmen of the airline. The loser was John Casey, who had been executive vice president. What to do with Mr. Casey? C. Edward Acker, then chairman of Pan Am and an old friend of Casey's (they had worked together at Braniff International), made Casey head of Pan Am World Services Corp. This subsidiary's main business was servicing the Kennedy Space Center in Florida. (Pan Am World Services operated the cafeteria, collected the garbage, and provided security guards at the space center.) The lesson of this brief history is simple: The Pan Am World Services subsidiary is, and has long been, a dumping ground for those who do not make it in the airline.

In 1986, Alert Management Systems Inc. was set up as a subunit of Pan Am World Services. Alert's job was to provide security services for airlines, including Pan Am. The following year, Terry Hickman needed a job. Hickman had long been a pilot for Pan Am, but had suffered a mild heart attack and was no longer medically qualified to fly. As a pilot, Hickman had been very active in union affairs and had dealt extensively—and had become fast friends—with Shugrue. (An ex-pilot himself, Shugrue had been in charge of union negotiations for the airline.) In June 1987, Hickman, with no background in security, was named head of Alert.

Although the word around Pan Am was that Shugrue had taken care of his old buddy Hickman by arranging his appointment to Alert, Shugrue disputes this. He states that others at Pan Am (subordinates of Shugrue) interviewed Hickman for the Alert job. Shugrue also argues that Hickman was fit for the job because he knew Pan Am well. Shugrue concedes that Hickman had no training in security, but says Hickman had "leadership qualities" because he had been a 747 captain.

Under Hickman, a West German firm named Securite was acquired, and its operations were merged with that of Alert. Pan Am's airline security in West Germany, previously handled by a private contractor, would now be handled by Securite, which was renamed Alert.

Along with Securite, Pan Am acquired its director of operations—Ulrich Weber. Weber became director of operations for Alert in

West Germany. Soon Pan Am headquarters in New York began getting anonymous letters—apparently from Alert employees—raising questions about Weber's activities. Pan Am launched an investigation, sending a team of auditors to Frankfurt, Alert's West German headquarters.

According to Pan Am, the auditors alleged that Weber had diverted Alert funds. Weber also was accused of various sexual indiscretions, including using nearly $5,000 in company funds to pay for a party at a Munich house of prostitution.

It was also discovered that Weber's background was not checked by Alert upon his appointment as director of operations. An investigation by an attorney suing Pan Am for the 103 bombing found that Weber had a previous criminal record in Illinois, where he once lived, for passing bad checks.

Hickman was asked to resign as head of Alert and did so in March 1989. Weber was fired from Alert for alleged financial misdeeds in June 1989.

Pan Am has maintained that Weber's various alleged activities did not degrade the airline's security in Frankfurt, where the bomb that blew up Flight 103 is believed to have been placed on board the jet. Following the bombing, however, the FAA sent an inspection team to Frankfurt, as well as to Heathrow Airport in London, a stop on 103's flight. At both Frankfurt and London, the FAA found a variety of loopholes in Pan Am defenses, including some of the same loopholes that led to the bombing of the Air India flight in 1985.

According to the FAA inspectors, Pan Am security personnel in Frankfurt identified five passengers about to board Flight 103 on the day of the bombing who should have been given additional screening. Such passengers normally are identified by asking them questions such as "Did you pack your own bag?" or "Are you carrying a gift for anyone?" If a passenger gives an answer that raises a red flag, then the passenger should be given greater scrutiny. But, as FAA inspectors discovered, none of the five passengers involved were looked at more closely. Contrary to the security requirement, neither the passengers nor their carryon items were searched. They simply boarded the plane.

The same was true of four interline passengers, who were connecting from another carrier to Flight 103. Although identified as subjects for further screening, the FAA discovered that the four were not searched, as required, nor were their carryon items or checked bags searched. These passengers also boarded.

In still another lapse of security on the same day, Pan Am personnel failed to conduct the required search of the 103's cargo bay prior to the loading of the luggage aboard the plane. (So far as is known, there is no hard evidence that any of these security lapses allowed the bomb to get aboard Flight 103, although investigators are still uncertain how the bomb did get aboard.)

Pan Am's Frankfurt security also failed on the same day for another flight, this one Flight 73 from the German city, the FAA found. Four passengers traveling from Budapest to Frankfurt, where they were to connect to Pan Am Flight 73 heading for New York, missed their Pan Am flight. But their bags had been checked through to the United States, and Pan Am baggage handlers in Frankfurt had put their bags aboard the Pan Am plane. Although the four passengers missed the Pan Am flight, their bags were not removed, and the bags were transported unaccompanied to New York.

Pan Am's Frankfurt security failed on the same day for still another flight, this one Flight 67. The FAA found that five passengers who were to travel on Flight 67 from Frankfurt to New York were off-loaded from the plane because one of them became ill. However, their checked bags were not removed from the jet, and these bags also traveled unaccompanied to New York.

At Heathrow, the FAA inspectors found a variety of infractions, including Pan Am's failure to give proper preliminary screening to 31 passengers, the repeated use of hand-held metal detectors (rather than the required search) to check items carried on board by passengers requiring additional screening, and Pan Am's failure to search a jet's cargo bay prior to loading baggage. The FAA proposed to fine Pan Am a total of $630,000 for the infractions. Pan Am has been contesting the fine.

Can Defenses be Improved?
The Case of the Terrorist's Toshiba

Ever since Pan Am 103 was brought down by an explosive hidden in a Toshiba radio, aviation authorities have been trying to figure out how to keep such bombs off jetliners. It has not been easy.

In July 1989, the FAA put out an emergency regulation on inspecting electronic devices, about six months after the Pan Am incident. The interim was filled with months of fierce debate among FAA officials and airline security directors about how to handle electronic devices, which include hand-held calculators, portable TV sets, and laptop computers, as well as radios. Even the final emergency regulation has loopholes that would enable a bomb to slip through, security experts agree. "We've been trying to develop the most reasonable and effective security system that we can," said Raymond Salazar, FAA director of security. But, he added in commenting on one loophole, "Ain't nothing perfect."

Aside from analyzing the effectiveness of the regulations, the process by which the FAA and the airlines hammered out the new rule offers some interesting insights. The FAA, under enormous public pressure to "do something" in the wake of the tragedy, suggests one sweeping rule after another. The airlines, upset that these new rules will disrupt operations and delay flights, protest mightily, and get the rules scaled back. The result is that the new rules will tighten security slightly, still allowing the planes to get off on time, but the real security dilemma remains unresolved, and the next bomb might easily slip through. Thus, an interesting question is raised: Is keeping the next bomb off a plane an impossible task?

The FAA was under especially intense pressure in this instance because of the discovery of four more bombs built by the same terrorist group, which were discovered in West Germany. All were concealed in electronic devices of one sort or another—a computer monitoring screen in one instance—and all contained barometric triggers, indicating they were meant for aircraft. Clearly, there were to be future targets.

Terrorists favor concealing bombs in electronic devices because the batteries, wiring, electrical, and barometric triggers needed for a bomb blend in easily with the parts of consumer electronic products. The FAA's first reaction was to consider an outright ban of all consumer electronic products.

On May 2, 1989, Transportation Secretary Samuel Skinner, in a speech at the National Press Club in Washington, floated a trial balloon. "The question on everyone's mind is what to do with electronic devices," he said. "A total ban of all such items on airplanes is an option we have to consider."

Skinner's trial balloon was soon punctured. Makers of laptop computers and other electronic gadgets phoned and wrote the Department of Transportation, which oversees the FAA, to express concern. More important, some foreign governments indicated a reluctance to go along with the ban. Because the major threat of bombs being put aboard airlines is in Europe, the Middle East, and elsewhere overseas, the cooperation of foreign governments would be crucial.

U.S. airline security directors also felt a total ban would be impractical because of passenger concerns. In addition to passenger complaints, there was the problem of defining the particular electronic devices to be banned. "Does the ban cover a small tape recorder...a hearing aid?" asked a security director. "Pretty soon we'd have a laundry list of things you could and couldn't bring on board, and that could be difficult for our airport screeners to handle."

With the total ban shot down, the FAA drafted a proposed regulation that called for a physical inspection of every electronic item brought on board. Airline security personnel were aghast. In meetings with FAA and Transportation Department officials, they said that inspecting each electronic item would turn airport security checkpoints into giant bottlenecks. Some passengers caught in long lines would miss their flights. If planes were held, that would cause flight delays, which are extremely costly for airlines and aggravating to the other passengers.

There also was an issue of personal safety for the airline screeners. The draft regulation ordered that during inspections, airline security persons should remove batteries from an electronic device. (Typically, the batteries in a device power a bomb's detonator; removing them would effectively disarm the explosive.) But what if the device were booby-trapped to explode when the batteries were removed, questioned airline security officials. The FAA rewrote the regulation. The new version read: "Ask the passenger to remove the batteries."

Salazar, the FAA security chief, maintained that the regulation was not rewritten to protect airline security personnel, but to make it easy to observe if the passenger becomes nervous when asked to take out the batteries, making him or her a suspect who should be further scrutinized. Of course, if a passenger is an unwitting carrier of a bomb, the passenger might readily remove the batteries.

It also is not clear how much the rewritten regulation would protect airline screeners. If a screener is standing too close when batteries are removed by a passenger from a booby-trapped device, one airline security director said, "I guess they both go up in smoke."

Some security directors mused about using the "Madrid technique" in these situations. At the airport in Madrid, a passenger with a suspicious device may be told to take it into a concrete room and remove the batteries, while monitored by video camera. This technique may have stemmed from an earlier explosion that killed an airport worker.

In its rewrite of the regulation, the FAA also deleted the section calling for inspection of each electronic device. Instead, airport screeners are required to ask a series of questions—"Did you receive this item as a gift? How long have you known this friend?" If the answers sound innocent, the item can be cleared without inspection. Passengers with suspicious answers will have their devices searched and be asked to remove the batteries. If a screener still is doubtful, the device is to be x-rayed. If doubts persist, a bomb expert is to be called.

Although the new regulation was scaled back from a total ban to inspection of all devices to the inspection of only some, government and airline officials argue that this does not amount to watering down security. "If you try to ban everything or search everything, you're spread too thin to catch the bad guy," says one airline official.

Nevertheless, security officials admit that the new regulation still may let a bomb slip through, even if the passenger seems suspicious enough to warrant a search of a device. When a device is opened for inspection, the new rule instructs screeners to look for parts "that do not match the majority of others used." However, one of the devices seized by West German police, a Toshiba Bom Beat 453 radio recorder, had internal parts bearing Toshiba labels and wiring diagrams that were actually part of the bomb mechanism.

Some security officials doubt that airport screeners will have the technical expertise to pick out such disguised parts, particularly as long as they are poorly paid and poorly trained. Given the vast range of consumer electronic products, the rapidity of product changes, and the number of internal electronic parts in any one item, it seems unreasonable to expect the average screener to be able to tell genuine parts from disguised parts.

There is another problem. Even if batteries are removed by the passenger, this may not necessarily disarm the disguised bomb. In the Toshiba Bom Beat, there was a second set of batteries—four tiny concealed cells that powered the bomb detonator.

For all the argument that has surrounded the new regulation, although security will be heightened somewhat, it will not be complete. It would not even stop a bomb, such as the one in the Toshiba (the current state of the terrorist's art), much less stop any devices that may be even more advanced or more cleverly concealed. Such devices may not be far from developed: Security men already are worrying that terrorists may develop a chemical trigger for a bomb, which would eliminate the need for the batteries and wires in detonating an explosive.

Is there a better way to provide security? Can intelligence agencies pick up clues to future bombings, and can the FAA then issue warnings to airlines that would help in blocking the terrorist operations? Here again, the answers are not reassuring.

The Role of Intelligence and FAA Warnings

"A terrorist group [is] considering an attack against a U.S. aircraft in either Guadeloupe or Antigua...."

"Unknown Palestinian terrorists are in possession of suitcase bombs...."

"*Hezbollah* members were planning to hijack a Pan Am or TWA aircraft in Greece, Turkey, Pakistan, India, or the Far East, at whichever location they deem the easiest."

These are all warnings issued secretly by the FAA to U.S. airlines throughout a 15-month period ending in March 1989. In an ideal world, the warnings would arrive with time to spare, alert airline security personnel would detect the bomb, and the plot would be foiled. Travelers would fly in safety.

However, a far different picture of the reality emerges after one examines the major FAA warnings disseminated to carriers and interviews current and former airline security officers. First, most of the warnings are so vague and lacking in detail that airline officials cannot take effective countermeasures. One warning merely recounted a British newspaper article purporting to describe a terrorist plot. And, in at least one case, when terrorists were discovered operating an improvised bomb factory in West Germany, three weeks passed before an FAA warning was dispatched to U.S. carriers—far too slow in the eyes of many security specialists.

"The other U.S. intelligence and law enforcement agencies consider the FAA a bunch of amateurs," says the security director of one carrier who previously served in an intelligence agency. Performance may be imperfect because the FAA is faced with a difficult and dangerous job, some security experts say. The warnings are sometimes vague because the FAA must depend on the military and the CIA for its overseas information—and military or CIA informants may themselves be vague or unreliable. In addition, when the FAA does get reliable information, it must perform a delicate balancing act: giving the airlines enough specifics to take meaningful action, but not so many details as to jeopardize an intelligence source.

"The FAA is on the horns of a dilemma," says Michael Ackerman, the former CIA agent who now advises corporate clients on security. "If the FAA warning is too specific and it somehow leaks, the terrorists are tipped off and they starting hunting for the person informing on them. But if the FAA is too vague, the bomb may get onto the plane and the plane may go down."

Monte Belger, the FAA associate administrator who oversees the agency's security department, says that "Our number one objective is to provide as much information as we can on known threats and new explosive devices to keep the airlines alert." When the agency gets good intelligence, he adds, it gets passed on "very rapidly" and "as specifically as possible as to time, location, and the nature of the threat." Belger also defends the FAA intelligence analysts as "extremely competent and proficient."

There is no doubt, however, that the FAA's warning system became the center of intense controversy following the bombing of Pan Am 103. Congresswoman Cardiss Collins released a study of FAA warnings, calling them "untimely," "inaccurate," and "almost completely devoid of effective and specific instructions for countering possible threats." Relatives of those who died because of the 103 bombing want the FAA warnings made public and are incensed that one warning that seemingly foreshadowed the bombing (that the U.S. government has subsequently called a hoax) was not disclosed to the public.

Prompted by the Pan Am bombing, the Transportation Department conducted a review of the FAA's warning system, but changed only minor, procedural aspects of the system. (One example of such a change is that airlines must now confirm to the FAA that they received the warning.)

The agency issued 27 warnings to airlines in 1988 and 7 more in the first quarter of 1989. The warnings take the form of written security bulletins telexed from FAA headquarters in Washington to the agency's principal security inspector for each carrier. The inspectors, in turn, deliver the message to the carrier's headquarters. When more speed is required, FAA staffers in Washington telephone airline security personnel directly. Once they receive a warning, airlines are supposed to heighten security as best they can.

There is no question that some FAA security bulletins are vague. On February 12, 1987, the agency sent out a bulletin that read in full: "As of late January, a terrorist group was considering an attack against a U.S. aircraft in either Guadeloupe or Antigua. The attack may come in the form of a bombing, but other forms of attack are also possible. FAA Comment: Although the location of the threat is fairly specific, other areas of the Lesser Antilles region must also be considered as potential target locations." The bulletin was sent to carriers serving the Caribbean; so far as is known, the plot was never carried out.

Other bulletins read like political science essays. One issued April 18, 1987, cited news reports about the U.S. Navy's destruction of an Iranian oil platform in the Persian Gulf; the assassination, apparently by Israelis, of Abu Jihad, a top official of the PLO; and the beginning of Ramadan, the Islamic holy month, "an emotional period for many Moslems." The bulletin continued: "The combination of Palestinian anger against Israel (regardless of who actually killed Abu Jihad); the tendency for anger against Israel to be transferred to the U.S.; probable Iranian...reaction to the conflict in the Persian Gulf and the beginning of Ramadan makes the current time frame especially dangerous. We believe U.S. carriers world-wide are at increased risk in the immediate future, although no specific information is available indicating what form a possible attack might take."

One FAA warning was based merely on an article in the *Independent*, a leading British newspaper, that said Iranian hit squads assigned to kill opponents of the regime would come to West European cities dressed as Iran Air flight attendants. Concerned that a hit squad using such disguises could gain access to "sterile" areas of airports, the FAA issued a warning April 7, 1987. It added that it was unable to confirm the existence of the plot.

In some cases, the FAA has relayed information from the military or the CIA that was admittedly from less-than-reliable sources. A bulletin sent out July 14, 1989, cited the warning "from another U.S. agency" about the *Hezbollah* members planning to hijack a Pan Am or TWA jet wherever it would be easiest. The bulletin cautioned that the warning was "according to unconfirmed information from a source with limited access whose reporting has been insufficient to establish a degree of substantiation."

"What was I supposed to do with this sort of stuff?" asked a retired security director of a major U.S. carrier. In more than a decade on his job, he said, "I never once got something [from the FAA] that I could act on. It was all too vague, too general." "We call these warnings CYA [for cover-your-ass]," adds the security director at another U.S. airline. He argues that the FAA, having received some threat information—however fragmentary—does not want to be in the position of not having passed it on, just in case something does happen.

Others are more sympathetic. "The FAA is trying to keep the airline people alert," says Ackerman, the former CIA agent. "Of course the agency runs the risk of crying wolf and nobody's paying attention." Billie Vincent, former chief of the FAA's security office, also defends the agency. "Some of these," he says, "are 'Hey, heads up, fellas,' and they're legitimate reminders."

Although Vincent agrees that some FAA security bulletins sound vague, he says that is because they may be sanitized to protect sources. He adds, "If we get information from a member of one of these terrorist groups, and if we somehow tip our hand, we may [in effect] kill the source."

Another difficulty, a former intelligence official notes, is that because other U.S. intelligence and law-enforcement agents view FAA officials as amateurs in the intelligence field, "often they don't trust the FAA." As a result, he says, "they can be very reluctant to give FAA their best stuff."

The FAA's Belger disputes that. The agency's intelligence staff has been built up in recent years to a tiny (about a dozen analysts), but very professional group, he says. Thus, he argues, "allegations of a lack of trust are probably unfounded." Belger also says security bulletins may be vague because his staff gets much of its information in classified form and must go through a complex process to declassify it. As for the bulletin recounting the *Independent* story, Belger says that was merely advisory, adding that "I wouldn't discredit the FAA for making sure the airlines were aware" of the article.

Yet another reason security bulletins can be vague is that it is so difficult to get precise information. Terrorist groups are often organized into cells of only a few people each, one of which may provide the bomb, another a safe house, and a third that may actually carry out the bombing. Only a few members of the third group—perhaps only one—would know the timing and the target. "You almost never find out that a guy is going to put a bomb on a TWA jet in Athens next Thursday," says one airline security director.

In the summer and fall of 1988, however, airlines heard the drumbeat of increasingly specific FAA warnings about terrorist actions. The warnings, which preceded the Pan Am bombing, have been the center of controversy because they were allegedly late, not specific enough, and were not made public.

On October 26 and 27, 1988, West German police raided several apartments in Frankfurt and Neuss that were being used by a terrorist group, the PFLP-GC. The police discovered a small arsenal: several machine guns, several dozen hand grenades, one Beretta pistol, rifle grenades, a bazooka, plastic explosives, TNT, blasting caps, and fuses. There were false passports and identity documents from Britain, France, Spain, Morocco, and Syria. And the police ultimately found several bombs, including one in a radio/cassette player. The police detained 16 suspects, ultimately arresting and charging only 2.

An FAA security bulletin issued November 2, 1988, cited several world developments as provocative, including parliamentary elections in Israel, a coming meeting of the Palestine National Council in Algeria, and legal proceedings against terrorists in the United States, West Germany, Malta, and France. The bulletin also noted "the arrest in late October of...alleged members of the PFLP-GC in West Germany on weapons charges." The bulletin said no more about the arrests.

Two days later, on November 4, 1988, the FAA issued another bulletin mentioning "the capture of numerous weapons and explosives" in the

PFLP-GC raid. But it still did not dwell on bombs; it emphasized the possibility of a hijacking of a U.S. airliner in Europe by a four-man Arab team traveling on passports from a Mideast nation.

Then, on November 17, the agency dispatched a bulletin devoted entirely to the PFLP-GC bomb hidden in a Toshiba Bom Beat 453 radio. About 300 grams of plastic explosive was enclosed in the metallic wrapper of a Tobler candy. For a trigger, the device contained a computer chip coupled to a barometric device, indicating that the bomb was meant to explode in an aircraft.

Although dated November 17—a Friday—the bulletin was not received by Pan Am until five days later, on November 22. Several people who have studied the sequence claim the FAA was inexcusably late. "The FAA dawdled for weeks before issuing vital information" about the bomb, Congresswoman Collins's study charged. Ackerman, who sends his own warnings to corporate clients, concurs. "The FAA was very slow; they should have had that information out much sooner." Meanwhile, the West German authorities had dispatched their own bulletin on November 10. It reached Pan Am in Frankfurt November 11.

FAA Associate Administrator of Security Belger responds that it was not until "several days" after the October 26 arrests that West German police technicians discovered there was a bomb in the Toshiba radio. He declined to say when or how the FAA got that information from West German authorities. Belger says that "once we got [the information], we put it out very rapidly."

Pan Am, meanwhile, was responding to the bulletin, but the airline, unfortunately, was focusing on carryon baggage, rather than checked bags. The airline's internal Security Task Force Wire NBR 23, dated November 23, 1988, referred to the PFLP-GC raid and the discovery of false passports from five nations. Among other things, the wire told employees: "You should include in your...screening process any individuals of apparent Arab ethnic background in possession of above documents [passports from the five nations] placing particular emphasis on those in possession of electronic devices such as radios/ cassettes/calculators, etc. as carryon baggage. Above devices should be closely examined and x-rayed." Pan Am, like most carriers, was not examining checked bags then. The bomb that brought Flight 103 down was in a checked bag.

On December 7, in an eerie development foreshadowing the Pan Am tragedy, the FAA issued another warning. Two days earlier, the agency stated, "an unidentified individual telephoned a U.S. diplomatic facility in Europe and stated that some time within the next two weeks there would be a bombing attempt against a Pan American aircraft flying from Frankfurt to the United States. An individual identified as [deleted] will...provide [a bomb] to an unidentified Finnish woman in Helsinki. The woman would unwittingly take the device to Frankfurt and eventually onto the U.S.-bound flight." The FAA said then that the reliability of the information could not be assessed; the United States subsequently called the phone call a hoax.

Conclusion

Passing through airport security in Frankfurt, at Heathrow, or even at Kennedy Airport in New York, a passenger encounters a seemingly formidable security apparatus. Questions are asked, handbags are searched, laptop computers are turned on to prove they really are computers, and passengers walk through metal detectors and are sometimes searched. There is an air of crisp efficiency.

But in the past, every time there has been an opportunity to look behind the scenes, as in the Air India bombing or the Pan Am 103 bombing, a far different picture emerges. Screeners are underpaid, undertrained, and often ineffective. The President's Commission on Aviation Security and Terrorism found that this state of affairs continues. At Baltimore-Washington International Airport, the Commission said in its 1990 report, Commission officials encountered "a screener's failure to identify an obvious explosive device in a briefcase put through the standard x-ray machine." The Commission's report added: "The screener was incapable of understanding questions posed to him in English concerning the extent of any training he may have received."

In addition to such problems, the FAA regulations under which screeners for U.S. carriers must operate are themselves the result of compromise, some probably necessary, but nevertheless leaving loopholes that would allow bombs to slip through.

One reason for this state of affairs is the structure of the security apparatus. The attackers, of course, have the advantage in that they alone know when and where they intend to strike. In light of this—and in light of their continued success—one would think the security apparatus would be organized in the most effective possible way. Not so.

In the pecking order of airlines, pilots are first class citizens, flight attendants and mechanics second class citizens, but security screeners are not even citizens at all because they do not work directly for the carrier. Demoralized by the fact that they do not get flight benefits (that the clerks working a few steps away do), underpaid and undertrained and doing a boring job, the screening staffs not surprisingly suffer enormously high turnover rates. Therefore, to expect a security screener to pick out a false part in a complex electronic mechanism such as tape recorder or video screen, contained in one of thousands of bags examined, is unrealistic.

The problem is compounded because of the fractured defense structure. Each airline must provide its own security screeners (and each has its own philosophy in so doing). Driven by economic incentives to hold costs down, the airlines only reluctantly upgrade their security apparatus.

Just as airline security people are without status in the airline industry, within the U.S. government, the FAA's security department too has long been considered second class. It has grown, but only in response to cataclysmic events such as the TWA hijacking and Air India bombing in 1985 and the Pan Am bombing of 1988. It is still a tiny part of the agency—a mere 500 persons in a 48,000-person bureaucracy.

The President's Commission found that the FAA's security office has failed to assume leadership on security issues, using only a reactive approach. The Commission blamed this on several factors: "A lack of visibility of the security function within the agency...insufficient staff resources for the security-related responsibilities; and a division of security responsibilities that leaves no one entity accountable."

At each airport, the security apparatus is further divided among several agencies: at J.F. Kennedy in New York, for example, among the security agencies represented are the FBI, the Drug Enforcement Administration, U.S. Customs, New York City police, Port Authority police, and multiple screening outfits hired by various U.S. and foreign carriers, as well as FAA offices.

Overseas, where the real threat is posed, the situation is even more complex and difficult to resolve. Although the FAA issues regulations requiring U.S. carriers to perform security functions one way, foreign governments often require that these functions be carried out another way. In fact, in many instances, U.S. carriers have little or no control over the security agencies they must use in foreign lands. Consider Belgium.

When FAA inspectors checked security at Brussels airport in 1989, the security agents hired by TWA flunked. Questions asked by ticket agents indicated that one passenger required intensive scrutiny, but the security firm working for TWA failed to x-ray his bags.

There was nothing TWA could do about this problem, however. The Belgian government insisted that TWA (as well as Pan Am and Northwest) use a local airport security company, Belgavia Security Systems N.V. "We have absolutely no control over Belgavia," said Charles Adams, a TWA senior vice president. "I mean, we can go out there and stand there and tell them what to do, and they don't pay any attention to us." Marc Pissens, general manager of Belgavia, blamed the security lapse on TWA, saying the airline would not hire enough Belgavia guards to do the job. He added that the problem has been solved because TWA increased its budget and hired more guards.

Foreign governments may require use of local firms for parochial reasons. Because security has become a big business, local firms are created to garner both the jobs and the revenues. Foreign governments also may require use of local firms in the name of sovereignty or because of honest differences with U.S. carriers about security techniques.

In Belgium, TWA, as well as Pan Am and Northwest, considered Belgavia inadequate and wanted to hire a security firm of their own choosing. But Monique Delvoy, spokeswoman for the Belgian Ministry of Transport, commented: "What we don't want is uncontrolled development of other private security firms, whose uniforms might be obtained by terrorists and used as a disguise."

Whatever the rationale, it is clear that foreign governments will pose major problems for U.S. carriers seeking to improve their security overseas.

If security remains poor, should travelers be notified of FAA threat warnings, as the survivors of Pan Am 103 have demanded? "If you can't protect us, as least warn us," says Bert Ammerman, whose brother died in the Pan Am bombing. Although such arguments have obvious emotional appeal, common sense appears to swing the argument in the opposite direction. Publicly announcing a threat would only tip off terrorists, who would then change the timing of their attack or their target. If the warning was accurate, terrorists would also learn that government officials have knowledge of their plans, and the terrorists would surely try to improve security within their own organizations. Of course, some threat notices (which often depend on unreliable sources) would be incorrect, and these, if made public, would only mislead travelers. The U.S. government has taken the position that threat notices to carriers should remain secret, to be dealt with by security professionals, and if security officials cannot guarantee the safety of a particular flight, it should be canceled. Although there may be some situations in which passengers getting on a plane should be informed of a threat—particularly when unusual searches or other procedures make it obvious that something is wrong—it seems reasonable that broad public dissemination of threats is generally counter-productive. When it comes to security, the public generally has to rely on the experts, no matter how inept they may be, just as when it comes to cases of serious illness, they must generally rely on doctors, despite their shortcomings.

Is there hope for improvement in airline security? Just as the Air India bombing had a traumatic effect on Canadian airline security, the Pan Am bombing is spurring an improvement in U.S. carrier security. Pan Am, for example, has disbanded Alert and folded all its operations into the airline itself, where it is likely to get more attention. In addition, Pan Am is now spending much more on training screeners and on more advanced x-ray machines. The FAA also has gotten more aggressive, prodding Pan Am and other carriers to improve security.

Another hope for the future are the TNA devices. Despite all their shortcomings, they represent a substantial advance in screening checked bags. The trouble is, the devices still may not be good enough. At TWA's terminal at New York's Kennedy Airport, where a TNA device is being tested, the machine is calibrated to detect only fairly large amounts of plastic explosives. Thus, the machine is set so that it would not detect a bomb of the size that brought down Pan Am 103. Unfortunately, however, if the machine were set to detect such small amounts, false alarms could soar to as much as 30 percent of bags. These bags would have to be reexamined, cutting the screening speed necessary to get flights out on time. For this reason, some airline executives, such as Robert Crandall, chairman of American Airlines, are adamantly opposed to the TNA machines.

Some scientists believe that other technologies may soon be developed that will improve both the detection rate and speed. French scientists say they are working on one technology that holds such promise. Whether it is TNA or another technology, however, there will still be major problems overcoming the reluctance of foreign governments to install the devices, particularly for any machine using a radioactive process. It will undoubtedly be years before effective and speedy bomb detectors are in place at airports around the world.

One remaining question is whether the whole security apparatus ought to be reorganized, with the U.S. government assuming the entire task, as U.S. carriers have advocated. It sounds like a good idea. Both the authority and the responsibility for carrying out security could be centralized in one agency. Without the cost pressures that now plague airlines, pay could be improved, training upgraded, and there could be opportunities for people to move up within the federal bureaucracy after a few years in the ranks as screeners. But for budget reasons, legal reasons, and political reasons, such a move seems unlikely. Even if the federal government were to suddenly develop a budget surplus, shed worries about legal liabilities for undetected bombs, and try to field its own force of screeners, most foreign governments would surely block them. As it is, many foreign governments either mandate that a local private security outfit be used by U.S. carriers or only grudgingly tolerate some other private concern hired by U.S. airlines. Having U.S. government officials operating security at their airports would be anathema to most foreign governments.

"Each country performs its own security—that's normal," says Jean Paul Emplit, a spokesman for the Belgian Airways Authority. "Would you accept Belgian security forces acting in the U.S.?"

Although much attention has been focused on Europe, the security situation is even worse in many Third World nations, particularly in Africa and Latin America. In those areas, security personnel are very poorly paid and easily bribed. Funds are lacking for security equipment such as fences around airport perimeters or modern x-ray machines. In addition, U.S. airline security officials view governments in Africa and Latin America as even more recalcitrant than Europeans when it comes to improving security. In Africa, the situation is so bad that the French carrier UTA takes along its own security team on every flight.

In sum, it is clear that there is no simple solution that can be used to resolve the multiple problems involved in airline security. There is no quick fix that can be uniformly applied at airports around the world. Airline security will continue in patchwork fashion, only fairly good at some airports, pretty poor at others. As it stands now, the U.S. carrier defense against aircraft bombs is a Maginot Line. It can and probably will be improved, but in the immediate future, it will almost surely remain vulnerable.

Notes

1. The FAA is often sued when air traffic controller errors contribute to a crash; these cases are usually settled quietly out of court.

2. After she was reported in news accounts to be under suspicion, May Mansur appeared at a press conference in Tripoli to deny any role in the TWA bombing. Thus far, no one has been formally accused.

5

U.S. Strategy toward Aviation Security: A New Look

Joseph W. Marx

U.S. airliners are increasingly the targets of brutal attacks from international terrorist organizations. In this case, two urgent matters cry out for the attention of U.S. policymakers. The most obvious matter is that U.S. airliners offer a convenient proxy for terrorists to strike back and avenge the actions of U.S. foreign policy. Equally troubling, but even more damaging in the long run, is the U.S. government's inability to adopt a coherent policy to assess this growing danger of airborne terrorism. Until the U.S. government develops a program that can address these problems, attacks directed against surrogate targets of the United States will likely increase.

This chapter analyzes the U.S. government's strategy toward aviation security. Given that the struggle to end air terrorism is beyond the scope of any realistic policy, this study does not purport to offer any utopian formula for winning the war against air terrorism. Rather, its premise is that a concerted effort—employing technical, political, and economic measures—can indeed be effective in lowering the level of airborne terrorism.

Three areas of U.S. aviation security will be discussed: the cost and effectiveness of aviation security technology, the ability of the United

States to ensure adequate security of U.S. carriers at foreign airports, and the problem of threat dissemination. These issues lie at the heart of any comprehensive aviation security program.

This chapter will first detail and evaluate recent technological innovations in aviation security. This will be followed by a discussion of the merits of the El Al security model—and, specifically, whether the United States should adopt a similar program. The problems that U.S. aviation authorities have in maintaining adequate security standards in foreign airports will then be addressed. Finally, the problem of threat dissemination will be examined, with emphasis on the difficulty of differentiating between those that are real and those that are spurious.

After examining these options in detail, the discussion will shift to a broader context. Possible scenarios for enhancing current aviation standards and potential solutions for new security programs will be considered as alternative strategies to the serious problem of terrorism in the air.

Aviation Security Technology

For U.S. air carriers, technology is the first line of defense against air terrorism. The more comprehensive a security system is, the less chance a potential terrorist has of sabotaging an airliner. Not only does state-of-the-art technology make a terrorist's job more difficult, it also has the added advantage of raising the confidence level of airline passengers.

This argument typifies U.S. strategy toward aviation security. On the surface, it seems logical. It states that increased technological breakthroughs can foil terrorist attacks against civil aviation targets. But the problem lies with the assumption on which this argument is based. That innovations in technology enhance aviation security is by now self-evident, but to assume that these breakthroughs offer any viable, long-term strategy against air terrorism is misleading.

It is misleading because the relationship between technology and terrorist strikes is direct, not absolute. Innovations in technology improve air security, but they are not in themselves a panacea against terrorism. A brief look at technological improvements in aviation security programs explains why. In response to an increasing number of airplane bombings in the early 1980s, private firms in California developed thermal neutron analysis. This process uses neutron bombardment of luggage to stimulate gamma ray emissions from the baggage, which are then analyzed for the presence of explosives.[1] The designers of this system claim that the TNA process can detect all commercial and military explosives, including C4, water gels, dynamite, and semtex, a plastic explosive formerly made in Czechoslovakia.[2] As an added feature, its makers allege a 95 percent accuracy rating, with a 4 to 5 percent false alarm rate.

Although this is a vast improvement on previous systems, it still falls short of the mark. What is needed is a higher detection deficiency—greater than 95 percent—and a lower false alarm rate. This is because with 10 billion pieces of luggage passing through major airports every year, even a 1 percent false-alarm rate would cause 100 million false alarms. Assuming 100 bombing attempts a year, this gives only one genuine response in 1 million alarms.[3]

Other drawbacks are also apparent. First, the TNA machine's size is mammoth. Thus, it is very bulky and requires constant supervision by trained personnel. Second, the machine emits low levels of radioactive isotopes. Its makers claim that these amounts are negligible, so small that they are not harmful to the operators of the machine or to the general public. But the very notion of machines emitting radioactive isotopes makes airline officials nervous.

There are other devices in production that have the potential to improve the effectiveness of airport security. A walk-through chemical detector ("sniffer"), which relies on chemiluminescence, is also available, but it requires about 30 seconds per passenger. The manufacturer is attempting to reduce the processing time to about six seconds per person, the point at which it would be acceptable to most airlines. The standard x-ray machine is also being upgraded to provide higher definition and colored displays for passenger screening. Later models may utilize infrared scanning to detect firearms.[4]

Yet many security experts remain skeptical about these technological innovations. Their skepticism stems from the experimental nature of this new technology. Brian Jenkins, a noted security expert at The RAND Corporation, remarked in an interview: "The new technology is still in the experimental stage. We are several years away from a reliable, practical means of bomb detection."[5]

Jenkins's point is well taken. Glossing over technical flaws in these systems only obscures the potential drawbacks to both air travelers and the airline industry. Again, the TNA machine illustrates this point. Once touted as the airlines' best hope against plastic and compound explosives, the designers of the TNA process are now reluctant to mention that their invention will trigger an alarm if certain foods or articles of clothing—which contain the same nitrates found in semtex and other explosives—pass through the machine. These articles can cause countless delays for passengers and endless headaches for airport authorities.

This underscores the point that technological advances are, by nature, only part of the solution. Any comprehensive assessment of aviation security must also take into account other variables. According to Richard F. Lally, security consultant with the Air Transport Association, the first variable that must be considered is that "the security system we have in place today was invented and placed in effect in January 1973 to combat a hijacking problem."[6]

In other words, the historical emphasis of aviation security has been focused primarily on the problem of hijacking. Thus, security systems were designed to detect pistols and knives carried by hijackers, not plastic explosives smuggled aboard by terrorists. To improve this antiquated system, Lally now argues that airlines must shift priorities away from the threat of hijacking to the reality of sabotage.

Although Lally's analysis has enjoyed currency among some aviation experts, it is only partially correct. Indications that the threat has shifted toward bombings and away from hijacking was evident in the early 1980s. The destruction of a Gulf Air jet in 1983 and a Air France jumbo jet in 1984 are just two examples that illustrate this trend.[7]

By spring of 1984, even the U.S. government recognized the growing threat of airline bombings and responded by circulating a secret memo outlining the potential danger it posed. The memo emphasized, in surprisingly stark terms, the threat to civil aviation. It stated that "the threat will not diminish and, in order to thwart any future attacks, the civilian aviation industry must take extraordinary measures....To some these measures may seem excessive, but they are not....We must be ready for them."[8] Clearly, the government wanted to convey the serious nature of the threat to the airlines. The irony then becomes why the airlines were so slow in responding to this growing danger.

Under closer scrutiny, the reason is obvious. In contrast to Lally's analysis, the problem was not so much that the perceived threat had not changed or that technology had not kept pace—at least partially—with terrorist measures. Rather, the problem was that other factors integral to airport security had been overlooked. Two specific points come to mind.

In the airline industry, the war to combat air terrorism has always taken a back seat to competition among air carriers. With the onset of deregulation in the 1980s, competition in the airline industry evolved into a Darwinian struggle. Victims of this struggle included carriers such as Braniff International and People's Express Airlines. Unable to maintain competition with their peers in the industry, these airlines have either gone into bankruptcy or have fallen prey to takeovers by stronger competitors.

This means that airline executives must constantly juggle the pressure to cut expenses with the need to maintain adequate security. And, all too often, resources allocated for security programs are lost in the shuffle of boardroom acrobatics and left to suffer the burdens of an overly competitive industry. As Wall Street journalist William Carley points out, "Airline executives have come under intense pressure to cut costs. One of their biggest cost items, sometimes as much as 40 percent of operating costs, is for personnel. Hence, the executives have tried hard to cut wage and benefit costs."[9]

The fact of the matter is that airlines already pay $500 million annually for security.[10] Unlike many of their foreign counterparts, U.S. airlines must absorb security costs themselves, or as they inevitably do, pass on those costs to the passengers. Naturally, when addressing the issue of costs, arguments have gone in both directions.

The airlines have long contended that because they are mere clay pigeons of the U.S. government, Washington should foot the bill. There is, of course, some credence to this argument. Most terrorists are interested in political blackmail of some sort; thus, to assert that terrorists are blowing up U.S. carriers for the sake of destroying the U.S. airline industry is tenuous, at best. Their actions are invariably directed at the foreign policy moves of the U.S. government.

Senator Frank Lautenberg of New Jersey, a member of the President's Commission on Aviation Security and Terrorism, sides with the airlines on this point. Says Lautenberg, "When our interests were threatened in the Persian Gulf, the President sent the Navy to protect the flow of oil....He didn't tell the oil companies to hire their own soldiers, to man their own navy."[11]

Yet, the other side of this argument is equally convincing. Although the airlines are correct in saying that the government's role in aviation security has been one of "too little, too late," they fail to mention that they want the best of both worlds. In other words, the airlines want the government to pick up the security tab, but they cringe at the sight of increased government oversight of their industry.

The airlines retort by pointing to the government's Aviation Security Trust Fund of $6.4 billion, a veritable war chest that could support some of these programs.[12] Long used to mask the federal budget deficit, airlines argue that these funds must now be channeled to the effort to combat air terrorism.

Congressman Dan Glickman of Kansas has been particularly vocal on this point. His disgust stems from the "tennis match" between the government and the airlines about who will fund security equipment, when the federal aviation trust fund, financed largely by taxes from the purchase of air tickets, has more than $6 billion. Glickman adds, "I don't think there's been a direct acknowledgement by our government that a threat against civil aviation is a threat against the U.S. government as much as a direct military threat from the Soviet Union."[13]

Glickman's point is valid, but the fact remains that airlines can do more to improve airport security as well. Using money from the aviation fund, adding surcharges to airline tickets, or developing some additional form of aviation tax are indeed steps available for combating the problem. However, these are only small measures, tantamount to putting a band-aid on a gunshot wound. Nothing substantial can be done until airline officials stop worrying about pinning the blame for past failures on the government and start examining their own worst enemy: namely, the incompetence of security officials behind these programs.

Carley has noted this troubling situation, highlighting the example of Pan Am security. Carley argues that Pan Am World Services was long a dumping ground for executives who no longer fit in the airline industry.[14] People with little interest in or experience with airline security measures were given responsibility for overall security operations. The message—as exemplified by the Pan Am 103 disaster—is painfully clear. Sloppy top level management trickles down to inefficient security systems. And the final result is that terrorists have an easier time in carrying out their missions.

In sum, poorly funded security programs are a problem. But well-funded programs with incompetent management can be even more dangerous because they create a false impression of security. Whatever the outcome, the fact remains that in their push for additional funding, airlines must also seek increased security expertise in combating air terrorism.

A further outgrowth of this problem is the abysmal training standards of security personnel. Not only is there no watchdog agency to ensure high standards of security competence, but the Federal Aviation Administration itself has concentrated the majority of its antiterrorism spending on technological development, rather than improvements in personnel.[15] There is no better example of how costly such a neglected security system can be than that of Pan Am's ground security at Frankfurt International Airport, preceding the bombing of Flight 103.

Pan Am's neglect is evident in the case of Samone Keller. At 19, Keller quit her job as a hairdresser to become a security officer for Pan Am's security group, Alert, in Frankfurt. Although Keller had received no formal training, four or five days after she started working, Keller was promoted to the position of supervisor with oversight of as many as 180 people.[16] Because the FAA does not run, let alone supervise, the day-to-day security operations of U.S. airliners, it is very difficult to safeguard against such acts of negligence.

Although the FAA does try to identify threats, outline security measures, enforce security regulations on an ad hoc basis, and provide technical support, the essential security responsibility still rests with the airlines. This means that the airlines are responsible for employee identification, background checks, aircraft protection, security of checked baggage, and the maintenance of law enforcement on the ground. Considering that most airlines are amateurs in the security business, this is, to say the least, a daunting task.[17]

The moral is simple. Airlines are in the business of flying planes, not securing airports. Thus, private firms are contracted to operate the complicated machinery. In most cases, this means that contracts go to the lowest bidder. "Salaries for security personnel are typically slightly more than what they would make at a restaurant. If say, a Burger King in Boston is paying $5 an hour, then we might be paying $6 to $6.50," says Steve Caldwell, marketing director for an airport security firm.[18]

To make matters worse, contractual security personnel (who are not airline employees) are not eligible for the free flight benefits granted by virtually every airline to its own employees.[19] Tshai Gonazi, one of the original developers of the TNA system, recognizes the magnitude of this problem. Gonazi argues that "the TNA detection system would require better trained security agents than those now employed. We'd like someone with an associate degree or a bachelor's degree, because the machine provides a lot of diagnostic information, and this must be interpreted in some cases."[20]

The importance of this point is crucial. The handling of such sophisticated equipment requires an alert, well-trained operator. Needless to say, a bored, underpaid, and poorly trained security operator is a terrorist's best friend.[21] According to Mike Pilgram, security consultant to major U.S. airlines, this is the very dilemma that U.S. airlines now face because the average airport security worker is "not sufficiently trained to identify diddly-squat."[22]

By now it is obvious that U.S. airlines make the mistake of placing great faith in technology alone to identify hijackers and bombs. Little attention is given to the quality of personnel operating these devices. But the problem is that advanced technology, used improperly, is not effective.

What are the alternatives for U.S. airlines? Is the problem simply that U.S. airlines need to modify their security procedures along the lines of other programs, such as the El Al model? Even if they did, would this be a practical way for the United States to combat air terrorism? To answer these questions, it is first necessary to examine the world's leader in airport security—El Al—and see why this company has been so successful in foiling terrorist attacks.

The El Al System

The cornerstone of the El Al security system is the opposite of the U.S. model; namely, human vigilance takes precedence over high technology.[23] This philosophy was adopted as a result of Israel's early experience with aviation terrorism. In the late 1960s and early 1970s, Israel was the target of bloody terrorist bombings. One episode of particular brutality was the 1972 bombing of the Ben Gurion Airport baggage area, in which more than 100 people were killed or wounded.[24]

Israel responded to this deadly threat by revamping its entire security apparatus. Central to this new system was that each boarding passenger arrive in time to be interviewed with both check-in and hand luggage in tow.[25] This has evolved into the now-famed "profile system," in which El Al security officials assess each passenger on an individual basis.

This process is the hallmark of distinction for the El Al system. As noted Israeli aviation expert Arik Arad described this system, "Most important [for El Al] is that its officials are able to concentrate on one passenger at a time—everybody is accountable and accounted for. If somebody has something to hide, he will show signs that our officers are trained to spot—he may sweat or fidget."[26]

Arad's statement is based on bitter experience. The Israelis have foiled at least 100 terrorist operations before the terrorists reached the airport. Some potential agents provocateurs have even been apprehended while purchasing tickets or casing an airport. On two occasions, Israeli officials stopped attacks by members of the PFLP-GC, the most likely suspects in the Pan Am 103 bombing.[27]

Without a doubt, vigilance has its rewards. Two of the most frequently cited incidents involving El Al illustrate this point more precisely. The first episode began in Zurich, Switzerland. In May 1978, a man appeared at the El Al airport counter in Zurich to board a 2 p.m. flight to Israel. During the grueling interview process, El Al security officials noticed something suspicious. It was when Swiss authorities x-rayed the man's suitcase for the second time—at the insistence of the El Al security chief—that a detonator was discovered in the handle, set to go off when the bag was opened.[28]

Yet, perhaps the most astonishing case of security vigilance happened four years ago at Heathrow Airport in London. Flight 016 was set to depart from London to Ben Gurion Airport outside Tel Aviv. During the interview process, a young Israeli security officer noticed something odd about an Irish passenger—Anne-Marie Murphy, who was traveling to Israel.

Pregnant, alone, and unable to offer any specific reason why she was flying to Israel, Murphy's travel plans seemed suspicious. El Al officials immediately suspected something dubious. Because no higher authority can overrule an El Al security officer once he suspects someone, officials pressed the matter further.[29] As it turned out, Murphy was the unwitting mule for the Syrian affiliated Abu Nidal group. She had been given an altitude bomb that was set to explode in midair. Because of alert security officials, the plot was foiled.

Although the profile system is the pride and joy of Israeli security measures, it is only the tip of a complex network of security procedures. Personal interviews are buttressed by a computerized data bank of terrorist profiles. This is further complemented by Israeli security agents—the equivalent of "sky marshals"—who prowl El Al's ticket counters looking for potential suspects or trouble spots. The quick response of these agents has been credited with preventing an even bloodier attack on the Rome and Vienna airports in December 1985.[30]

The story does not end here. The cargo bays of El Al airliners have been reinforced to withstand the impact of a bomb explosion. In 1972, when a bomb hidden in a tape recorder exploded in flight, the reinforced walls of the cargo bay contained the damage and the plane landed safely in Rome.[31] In addition, all El Al jets are equipped with a missile detection system and can eject flares to divert surface-to-air missile attacks.

That El Al's security system is in a class by itself is by now axiomatic, but the fact remains that U.S. airliners have not adopted similar measures. A casual observer of airport security might complain that U.S. airliners have been lax in implementing similar measures. Many would wonder whether U.S. officials will do everything possible—especially in light of the Pan Am 103 disaster—to prevent another catastrophe in the future. Disasters such as Pan Am 103 would logically point to the creation of a similar program for U.S. airlines.

The attempt to draw a direct correlation between El Al and U.S. carriers would be misguided, however, because the scope of the threat and the means to address it are different. To start with, El Al operates only 20 aircraft, which are funded by the government, with flights to only 31 cities. In contrast, the United States has 230 scheduled and charter carriers, which operate more than 4,000 flights a day to nearly 600 airports around the world. Although a fair percentage of these are domestic flights—in which the threat of bombing is minimal, while the threat of hijacking is real—U.S. airliners still offer terrorists a broader range of targets than do El Al aircraft.

An additional point of contention for U.S. airlines are the possible delays that a more in-depth security system would require. Of the world's billion annual airline passengers in 1987, El Al carried a total of only 1.4 million. And El Al's passengers, a relatively homogenous group, are more willing to accept the delays and inconveniences that go with effective security.[32] Whether or not the incorporation of measures such as the "profile system" would cause endless delays for U.S. air passengers is questionable. Considering that international travelers must usually check in two hours in advance, it is possible that this system—if only on a limited basis—would work.

The purpose of comparing El Al security measures with those of U.S. airlines is not to excuse U.S. airlines from their questionable safety records, but to illustrate the inherent difficulty of integrating El Al's security model into the U.S. system. And, even before attempting to implement a new strategy, the United States needs to grapple with two other problems that have plagued aviation security programs: security procedures for foreign airliners flying to the United States and threat dissemination.

Security at Foreign Airports

If United States is to be successful in confronting the growing trend of air terrorism, then joint cooperation with foreign airports and air carriers is a must. The idea of raising only the standards of U.S. security measures would be tantamount to posting a policeman at every other street corner of a dangerous neighborhood. There would simply be too many loopholes for terrorists to slip through the system. In response, the FAA has been at the forefront of this issue and has recently released a list of security requirements for foreign airports and airliners serving the United States.

The main point was the following: Foreign airlines operating in the United States will be required to submit their security programs to the FAA for review and acceptance. The rationale behind this measure was to ensure that the 111 foreign airlines currently serving U.S. airports have adequate security measures to protect civil aviation against criminal acts of violence.[33] As a corollary, the FAA mandated the installation of a number of TNA machines in foreign airports that were particularly susceptible to terrorist attacks or that had been the target of bombings in the past.

In the words of Transportation Secretary Samuel K. Skinner, "The new requirements apply to flights by United States carriers from cities in Europe and the Middle East, where the risks of terrorism are considered to be highest. They do not cover flights within the United States or from the United States to overseas destinations."[34]

It would be an understatement to say that this new policy sent a shockwave through foreign transportation agencies. Every time the United States tries to impose its measures on foreign airports, cries of encroachment ring out. In the eyes of David Kydd, spokesman for the International Air Transport Association in Geneva, "This policy has put the European governments in a tizzy, because it not only seems to assume that non-U.S. airlines are at a higher level of risk than their own government consider them to be, but also raises an important legal point as to the extraterritorial application of a U.S. edict."[35]

To be sure, calls for a unilateral extension of U.S. authority over foreign airports are not conducive to promoting cooperation among various transportation agencies. Although Secretary Skinner's message seemed harsh to other departments, the focus of his remarks were on target: Governments must begin to cooperate with one another and share information if the struggle against air terrorism is to yield some success.

Skinner alluded to this at a conference with European officials in 1989. He said, "This is not an attempt by me to impose unilaterally...significant requirements upon foreign governments that they don't find acceptable...but at the end of the week West Europeans are going to know that America has a transportation secretary who is concerned about these [security] measures."[36]

The British, although a bit miffed by the tone of Skinner's statement, were the most sympathetic to the U.S. move. The reason is simple: Many security officials fear that the post-1992 air traffic network will be as vulnerable to terrorist infiltration as the human body is to a virus infection.[37] Recognizing from past experience—that is, the Flight 016 experience—the danger of air terrorism, Britain's transportation agency wants to ensure an adequate defense against future attack.

The British—with the French in tow—have stated that they would be happy to review U.S. security measures, but note that the ultimate decision concerning security operations lies with them. In this regard, it seems that Skinner's initiatives have worked. Although it remains to be seen whether countries will adopt the FAA's measures (until now, no foreign governments have), the idea has spawned cooperation among various transportation agencies.

In the case of Britain, France, and the United States, one immediate benefit springing from closer transatlantic cooperation has been a greater sharing of information among the security and intelligence services.[38] This is taking the form of look-out posts, for example, where officers will screen passengers on transatlantic flights against lists of suspects prepared by the U.S. and British intelligence services. The link is likely to be formally extended to include Interpol in the future.[39]

The urgency of these measures becomes more apparent when comparing the varying degrees of security measures at Europe's major airports. In Paris, security at Orly and Roissy-Charles de Gaulle is directly controlled by the government through three of its police agencies.[40] Although the Americans—and the Israelis—use their own security forces, nearly every other airline uses French security. The obvious problem with this arrangement is that there are conflicts between French security forces and private security contractors.

A noble solution for the Americans might be to cede authority to the French security forces on the condition that the United States can play an active—although not controlling—role in security operations. Considering the low standards that U.S. security forces have exhibited in the past, this seems to be a viable option, both to ensure proper security and to come to terms with the French government's desire to control security on its own soil.[41]

Across the border in neighboring Germany, events have taken a different shape. Although the Germans have not adopted the FAA's recommendations for security standards, they have been more sympathetic to the FAA's security concerns. In particular, the Federal Transportation Ministry in Bonn has agreed to review U.S. security standards for Lufthansa flights into the United States. For the United States, this is at least a sign that the Germans are willing to cooperate.

Along the Mediterranean, the Italians have perhaps had the most vigilant airport security force. Controls in Rome begin even before passengers reach the airport, with police monitoring traffic into and out of intersections. Italian security forces also patrol international departure gates with German shepherds trained to smell contraband and explosives. Although this technique may be somewhat unconventional, it tends to intimidate passengers and may be effective in ferreting out terrorists.[42]

Across the Adriatic, lapses in security at Athens airport are appalling. Athens has the distinction of being the only European airport declared unsafe by U.S. security officials. Although security officials at this airport claim that there are eight guard posts staffed 24 hours a day, a reporter traversed Olympia Airport and found evidence to the contrary. Throughout the day, Greek police officers, some of them drivers of armored trucks or agents of private security firms used by airlines, were found congregating around coffee tables.[43]

These weak links at foreign airports deal a damaging blow to any coordinated security effort. If, for example, Germany, France, Great Britain, and other countries maintain a minimum standard of security, and other airports do not, then the system can be circumvented through "soft spots" like Greece. Here, and in other areas with lax security, terrorists may try a new tactic: infiltrating their members into airport security organizations. Without adequate precautions, terrorists could then wreak havoc on airliners from within the system.

In this case, the International Civil Aviation Society has agreed to help finance security improvements in underdeveloped countries. However, unless countries such as Greece, as well as many Third World nations, exhibit more vigilance in complying with these regulations, the effort will be for naught.

Aside from the everyday security measures that airports must implement, another problem that plagues international airports is threat dissemination. The difficulty of deciding when to notify passengers of a threat must constantly be weighed against the possibility that the threat itself is spurious. The final step that U.S. officials must examine before formulating a strategy, then, is their policy toward threat dissemination.

Threat Dissemination

Picture the following chain of events and imagine the problem it causes for FAA officials: Narco-terrorists in Colombia are threatening to bomb a U.S. aircraft flying from South America to the United States within the next month. There are no other details except that the intended strike is in retaliation for the U.S. government's harassment of drug traffickers. Or consider another possibility: Palestinian terrorists possess a radio bomb filled with semtex. Sources point to a possible attack on a U.S. aircraft leaving Turkey, Greece, the Middle East, India, Pakistan, or Egypt.[44]

These types of security bulletins are common for the FAA. Ideally, security officials would trace terrorists' threats to their origin, hunt them down, and destroy their base of operation. Passengers would then fly safely to their destination, unaware of the threat. In reality, the opposite is true. The FAA is very unlikely to stumble across a precisely detailed warning. More often, security officials have to contend with an endless array of vague reports, which make it almost impossible to determine—let alone track down—the threat. As Brian Jenkins points out, "The problem with this [threat information] is that it is difficult to determine which terrorist threats are credible and which are not."[46]

The warnings are often vague because the FAA must depend on military or CIA information, and informants for these organizations are often vague in describing the details of the warning.[47] And when the FAA does get reliable information, it must perform a delicate balancing act: giving the airlines enough information to act on specific cases, but not enough to jeopardize its intelligence source.[48]

Deciding between betraying a source by giving specific details about the threat and jeopardizing the safety of an aircraft by remaining vague about the threat is not an enviable task for the FAA. Nonetheless, it is a dilemma that the FAA faces on a daily basis. Monte Belger, the FAA associate administrator, puts security policy in more straightforward terms: "Our No. 1 objective is to provide as much information as we can on known threats and new explosive devices to keep the airlines alert."[49] He adds that when the agency gets solid information about a potential attack, the information gets passed on "very rapidly" and "as specifically as possible as to time, location, and the nature of the threat."[50]

One of the obstacles that the FAA must overcome is its lack of credibility in the eyes of other intelligence agencies. This often means that agencies such as the FBI and CIA play a game of cat and mouse, often refusing to divulge their best information, either because they are working on the same project or because they view the FAA as a second class intelligence organization. One CIA official put it more bluntly: "Other law enforcement agencies view the FAA as a bunch of amateurs."[51]

Belger is quick to retort, defending the professionalism of his organization. He argues that the FAA's intelligence staff is a very sound group, but faced with a logistical nightmare. Although it is true that the magnitude of information that the FAA must digest on any given threat is quite large, the fact remains that other variables come into play that add further misery to the FAA's task.

"To publicize every threat," says terrorism expert Neil Livingstone, "would allow terrorists to pull the chain of the airline industry merely by making a telephoned threat."[52] Not only would this policy allow terrorists to hold sway with the airline industry, it could also ignite a chain of copycats, who could easily paralyze the airline industry. Paul Bremer, President Ronald Reagan's ambassador-at-large for counterterrorism, adds that "to publicize every threat would encourage copycat threats and actions, initially cause panic and disrupt air service and, in the end, cause indifference to the alerts."[53]

Yet another reason why security bulletins are so vague is that, more often than not, only fragments of information filter down to the FAA about possible attacks. An interesting case in point: One FAA warning was based merely on an article in the British newspaper, the *Independent*, that itself was probably based on hearsay.[54] The article intimated that terrorists disguised as Iran Air flight attendants would come to a West European city and carry out a bombing against an American airliner. There were no further details elaborating the nature of the threat. "What was I supposed to do with this sort of stuff?" asks the recently retired security director of a major U.S. carrier.

U.S. government policy toward threat dissemination has traditionally been closemouthed. The Bush administration has argued steadfastly that releasing every threat against civil aviation targets would be counterproductive. As the architect of this policy, Samuel Skinner quipped at a news conference in 1989: "We [the administration] disagree with the policy of releasing all threats, and believe it would be flatly at odds with a proper discharge of our responsibility to ensure safety in the skies. Publication of all threats will undoubtedly increase the number of hoax threats."[56]

The key point of contention with this policy is that by not announcing threats, air travelers become innocent victims of terrorist actions. In effect, they become surrogate targets of U.S. foreign policy actions. But the obvious recourse of publicizing every threat, which in turn would allow terrorists and cranks to hold the airline industry hostage, also fails to offer a viable solution. The airlines, in conjunction with the FAA, should only release information concerning a possible bombing when the threat seems credible. This is the juncture at which the U.S. government must join the hunt. To ensure the safety of air passengers, the Bush administration must work toward developing a strategy that narrows the ability of a terrorist organization to bomb civilian airliners.

Conclusion: A New Strategy

In late 1989, the FAA produced a report that demonstrated a renewed effort at tackling the problem of terrorism in the air. The tragic loss of Pan Am 103 revealed that more aggressive measures were needed to combat the sophistication of airborne guerrilla warfare. After reviewing security procedures at major airports around the world and at home, the FAA came up with a list of immediate recommendations to stem the tide and lethality of air terrorism. They included the following:

- 100 percent x-ray or physical inspection of all checked baggage;
- prohibiting passenger access to checked baggage after security inspection;
- thorough questioning of passengers who meet certain criteria and others, selected at random, all to undergo screening;
- positive matching of all passengers and checked baggage.

As of March 16, 1990, these measures have been amended to include the following for security personnel:

- All security personnel must speak English and have high school diplomas or equivalent work experience.
- All must pass a test showing they have an aptitude for the job. Also required are drug tests and background checks.
- All personnel must pass a hands-on test after completing a 12-hour training program. (Prior to this, the FAA had not set a minimum number of hours for training.) Supervisors will also get eight hours of special training.[58]

As a first step, these initiatives are encouraging. But the long-term outlook is such that air terrorism must be treated as a special kind of warfare if any strategy is to prove effective. And, one wonders if this issue would have received so much attention, had it not been for the efforts of the Lockerbie family groups who have maintained a steady barrage of criticism against the airline industry.

So the question becomes: How does one combat air terrorism? In developing a formal approach, several things need to be kept in mind. First, the quality of security management, personnel, and training has often been sacrificed in the interests of cutting costs. This is a result of the huge commercial pressures that airlines face to minimize operation costs to beat out the competition. In the era of cutthroat competition, it takes a brave airline to risk putting itself at a commercial disadvantage by imposing more exacting security standards while other airlines take a chance and cut corners.[59] Thus, the airline industry would benefit greatly from a supranational organization to hand out fines and to enforce security procedures—like the FAA does—in situations in which lapses of security occur.

At first glance, this argument would be cast aside as pure rhetoric; it is an accepted fact that nations are very reluctant to cede sovereignty of their security operations to an outside organization. Nonetheless, the benefits of such a plan outweigh the drawbacks and, thus, merit a closer look. First of all, there is little point in upgrading the airports in the United States, Great Britain, and Germany into shining examples of security efficiency, if, in the meantime, terrorists are able to find numerous weak links in the international system, such as the airports of some Third World countries.[60]

A possible body to perform this role would be the International Civil Aviation Organization (ICAO). To begin with, it should establish a fund—through taxes on airline tickets or government subsidies—to provide loans and grants to poorer nations to upgrade their antiquated systems and to more advanced nations to continue research into the evolving nature of the threat. One reason such a program has never been developed is because the issue of air terrorism is by nature ephemeral. The bombing of an airplane brings terrorism into public eye, but— especially in the case of U.S. public opinion—only for a short time.

This is arguably the Achilles' heel of aviation security efforts. Until public sentiment is sufficiently centered on dealing with the threat of aviation terrorism, it will be difficult to establish an international agenda to confront this problem. As Carley points out, it will probably take a number of particularly deadly attacks, within a short span of time, to raise the public's awareness of the severity of the threat of air terrorism.[61]

To keep attention focused on this problem, the ICAO came out with a number of proposals to condemn the acts of aviation terrorism. In a meeting in 1989, ICAO officials decided on the following terms:

- the global condemnation by ICAO of acts of unlawful interference against civil aviation, like the sabotage of Pan Am 103;
- the unanimous agreement of all ICAO member states to expedite the review and implementation of stricter security standards across the world;
- recognition of the need to impose more stringent security checks in areas of increased security threats;
- the immediate call for all countries to adhere fully to existing security standards;
- the joint decision to expedite research and development on detection of explosives and on security equipment; and,
- an agreement to explore the development of an international regime for the marking of explosives and detonation devices to increase detection.

This is only the beginning. In the past, various proposals from security experts—most recently from the President's Commission on Aviation Security and Terrorism—have fallen woefully short of the mark. Now, more stringent measures are needed.

One step would be to strike back against state sponsors of terrorism where it hurts—on the economic front. Without these sponsors, terrorist groups could not lash out with impunity. In this regard, tough economic and aviation sanctions against state sponsors of terrorism would bring home the message that the price of state-sponsored terrorism is not affordable.[62] This is especially the case with the "club of four" in the Middle East—Libya, Syria, Iran, and Iraq. If these four countries seek Western economic assistance, then they must follow the Western rules of the game.

Aviation sanctions that severe ties between the terrorist state and the rest of the world would be a further effective means of dealing with these countries. This could be done by convincing all nations that have not already done so to ratify and implement the Tokyo, Hague, and Montreal Conventions (which are security annexes to the Chicago Convention, the basic international civil air transport agreement) and ICAO Annex 17. The effect of these agreements is to remove terrorists from their bases of operation and to deny them sanctuary after operating. Again, there are obvious limitations to the United States' ability to influence the "club of four," but as evidenced by the UN blockade of Iraq, even these countries are not totally immune to U.S. and international pressures.[63]

In a related matter, enhanced cooperation among foreign intelligence agencies would go a long way toward coordinating efforts to combat international air terrorism. By pooling available intelligence resources, agencies would be able to increase their effectiveness in clamping down on international terrorism generally.

Next, security officials should do everything possible to make airports safe. In general, a secure airport is one that controls its perimeter and access to secure areas, inspects all baggage, matches all passengers to their baggage before flights, and ensures that all ticketed passengers are accounted for prior to takeoff. A 1986 Government Accounting Office (GAO) study of Dulles International Airport found that 2,000 of the 9,000 airport employee badges issued there could not be accounted for. Other airports, such as Washington National Airport, have additional weaknesses, such as too many access doors to the flight line and no perimeter fencing from some approaches.[64]

All of these suggestions point to the potential value of having a central office in the U.S. government to fund and coordinate research pertaining to terrorism. At present, counterterrorist research and development—let alone aviation security research and development—is funded at very low levels.[65] Perhaps if this were combined with counternarcotics research and development operations, the proposal would then be more attractive to legislators.

Because the threat of aviation terrorism is cyclical, the sad fact remains that governments lack the political will to implement such measures. It is inherently difficult to garner any long-term support for aviation security proposals. As a result, strategies to confront terrorists and state sponsors of terrorism are usually filled with empty promises. The scene is all too familiar. Immediately following an airline bombing, legislators jump at the chance to voice their outrage, only to retreat when it comes time to vote for more stringent measures.

The United States must, therefore, take the lead in developing a global effort to address aviation terrorism. This is necessary because current measures (proposed by the ICAO and the FAA) are not sufficient enough to deter international terrorist organizations from carrying out attacks against civilian airliners. Without the firm resolve to learn from past attacks and work toward a new strategy, tragedies such as Lockerbie will continue to fill the pages of history.

Notes

1. Conversation with Chris Mellon and Tom Maertens.
2. David Field, "Jet Bombing Prompts FAA, Britain to Upgrade Security," *The Washington Times*, December 28, 1989, p. 8A.
3. Fred Singer, "Machines Won't End Air Terrorism," *The Wall Street Journal*, June 20, 1989.
4. Conversation with Chris Mellon and Tom Maertens.
5. Neil C. Livingstone and David Halevy, "Is It Really Safe to Fly?" *The Washingtonian*, May 1989, p. 245.
6. Laura Parker and David Ottaway, "The Weak Link in Airline Security," *The Washington Post*, April 3, 1989, p. A1.
7. Ibid.
8. Ibid.
9. William H. Carley, Paper presented at Aviation Security Conference at The Johns Hopkins Foreign Policy Institute, March 1990.
10. Eric Weiner, "Who Is Going to Pay for Airport Security?" *The New York Times*, September 5, 1989, p. 4E.
11. Ibid.
12. Stephanie Gibbs, "Billions Unused in Drive to Tighten Airport Security," *The Post Standard*, 1989.
13. Jennifer Dorsey, "State Department Defends Airlines' Policy on Terrorist Threats," *Travel Weekly*, February 22, 1989.
14. Carley, Aviation Security Conference.
15. John H. Cushman Jr., "Airport Security: Slowly Getting Tighter," *The New York Times*, May 15, 1989, p. 1.
16. Tom Foster, "Frankfurt Tightens Up," *The Post Standard*, December 19, 1989.
17. Douglas W. Delp, "Terror in the Skies," *The Rotarian*, November 20, 1989, pp. 17-21.
18. "Flight 103: What We Must Do Next to Eliminate Risks," *Conde Nast Traveler*, March 1989, p. 36.
19. Carley, Aviation Security Conference.
20. Field, "Jet Bombing," 8A.
21. Delp, "Terror in the Skies," 17-21.
22. Livingstone and Halevy, "Is It Really Safe to Fly?" 245.
23. Ibid., 160-250.
24. Ibid., 243.
25. "Flight 103," 2.

26. Ibid.

27. Livingstone and Halevy, "Is It Really Safe to Fly?" 243.

28. Ibid.

29. Ibid., 161.

30. Ibid., 243.

31. Ibid.

32. Ibid.

33. U.S. Department of Transportation, *Skinner Says FAA Adopts New Security Rules for Foreign Airlines Serving U.S.*, DOT 24-89, March 14, 1989.

34. John H. Cushman, Jr., "Airlines Ordered to Tighten Security Measures," *The New York Times*, June 23, 1989, p. 6A.

35. Timothy Harper, "U.S. Air Security Push Draws Foreign Flak," *The Chicago Tribune*, April 16, 1989, p. 5.

36. Lee May, "U.S.-European Talks to Focus on Air Terrorism," *The Los Angeles Times*, April 25, 1989, p. 1.

37. Guy Norris, "Security Concerns Across the Atlantic," *Aerospace Review*, July 1989, p. 693.

38. Ibid., 693-694.

39. Ibid.

40. Cushman, "Airport Security," 1.

41. Norris, "Security Concerns Across the Atlantic," 693-694.

42. Personal Experience of the Author.

43. Cushman, "Airport Security," 3.

44. William H. Carley, "Terrorism Alerts: The FAA's Dilemma," *The Wall Street Journal*, April 3, 1989, p. 2.

45. Ibid.

46. E.J. Dionne Jr., "The Limits of Risk," *The New York Times*, March 20, 1989, p. 1.

47. Carley, "Terrorism Alerts," 2.

48. Ibid., 1B.

49. Ibid.

50. Ibid.

51. Ibid.

52. Douglas Jehl and Robin Wright, "U.S. Confirms Hijack Alert May Revise Warning Policy," *The Los Angeles Times*, March 27, 1989, Part 1.

53. Jennifer Dorsey, "House Approves $100 Million for Bomb Detectors," *Newsline*, October 5, 1989, p. 15.

54. Carley, "Terrorism Alerts," 1B.

55. Ibid.

56. Jonathon H. Cushman, Jr., "Flying Blind with Few Sources on Security Threats," *The New York Times*, May 1, 1989, pp. 1-30.

57. U.S. Department of Transportation, *Semiannual Report to Congress on the Effectiveness of the Civil Aviation Security Program*, July 1, 1998-December 31, 1988, pp. 1-2.

58. Lori Sharn, "FAA Tightens Security Rules at Airports," *USA Today*, March 7, 1990, p. 1.

59. Carley, Aviation Security Conference.

60. Paul Wilkinson, "Aviation Terrorism and the Changing Threat," *Interavia Aerospace Review*, July 1989, pp. 689.

61. Carley, Aviation Security Conference.

62. Wilkinson, "Aviation Terrorism," 688-691.

63. Conversation with Chris Mellon and Tom Maertens.

64. Ibid.

65. Ibid.

6

Mercenaries of Ideology: Turkey's Terrorism War

by Bilge Criss

During the 1960s and 1970s, Turkey suffered the highest, most prolonged level of internal terrorist violence in modern times. Groups from the Left and Right fought each other and the state, disrupting society until they were crushed following the 1980 military coup. These events remain controversial. Some analysts see them as a Soviet effort to destabilize Turkey. Yet whatever the source of ideological influence or financial aid that flowed to Turkish terrorists, the phenomenon was rooted in the domestic political climate and the government policies designed to cope with the crisis.

Although the majority of Turkish people did not condone terrorism, ideologues have had a large pool of unemployed, unskilled, and uneducated manpower from which to draw militants. Conservative governments chose to rely on rightist militants to suppress leftists. In addition, the failure of the Turkish constitution to impose checks and balances on the National Intelligence Agency, General Staff, and National Security Council had discouraged cooperation between military and civilian authorities in combating terrorism.

The political history of modern Turkey has been marked by the struggle to balance the forces of authority and dissent.[1] This fragile balance was upset by an authoritarian single-party regime in the 1920s, 1930s, and 1940s; by the failure of the first experiment in multiparty democracy in the 1950s; by the military coups of 1960, 1971, and 1980; and by martial law, military tribunals, a number of death penalties, countless prison sentences, as well as a ban on books, journals, and established political parties. As a result, the supremacy of the Turkish parliament was severely damaged. Meanwhile, coupled with economic crises, mounting inflation, population growth, and unemployment, an unprecedented threat to the state has appeared—terrorism.

Ideological Background

Beginning with the declaration of the Turkish Republic in 1923, the Republican People's Party (RPP), established by Mustafa Kemal Atatürk and his colleagues, was the single ruling party until 1950. Atatürk's timing was well chosen for social engineering. Following the Turkish war of independence (1918-1922), he was considered the nation's hero and savior. Although some orthodox Muslims considered it blasphemy to be ruled by secular—as opposed to divine—laws, their opposition was to no avail. Experimentation with multiparty democracy in 1924 and 1930 failed because the new parties' opposition to the tenets of the Turkish revolution was perceived to be harmful. Those principles included laicism, statism, revolutionism, populism, nationalism, and republicanism, with laicism being the most radical principle of all. For the first and only time in history, a predominantly Muslim country had adopted secularism.

Under Atatürk, religious schools were regulated by the directorate of divinity in the state bureaucracy. Atatürk had the calls to prayer recited in Turkish. This was perceived as yet another act of sacrilege by some members of the Muslim religion, which had failed to undergo a reformation or a renaissance of its own. However, under the benevolent authoritarianism of Atatürk, there was little overt opposition to these reforms. He, in turn, believed that rational thought would prevail, and, in time, all opposition to secularism would die a natural death. This was not to be the case. In 1950, the Democratic Party (DP) government resumed Arabic calls to prayer, and the number of religious schools increased.

Following Atatürk's death in 1938, President İsmet İnönü ruled Turkey as the "national chief." During the turbulent years of World War II, İnönü managed to prevent Turkish involvement in the fighting. In

1944, he moved against rightists and leftists. When a rightist "nationalist" theoretician accused İnönü's minister of education and the prime minister of harboring Communists, İnönü had some "nationalists" taken into custody on charges of forming a racist and revanchist pan-Turkish association. One year later, all charges were dropped, and the "nationalists" were acquitted. This faction included professors, journalists, and young officers, among whom was a Lieutenant Alparslan Türkeş, the future leader of the Nationalist Action Party.[2] Leftist faculty members were also purged.

In 1945, Soviet dictator Joseph Stalin's demand for Turkish territory, his subordination of all foreign Communist parties, and the Cold War era engendered a distaste for and fear of socialism and communism. Thus, neither Russian history nor socialism or communism was taught as part of the curricula in the universities and the war academy. Instead, the subject was monopolized by radicals. During the 1940s and 1950s, romantic leftist literary figures such as the author Sabahattin Ali, the poet Nazım Hikmet, as well as leftist journalists, educators, and politicians were tried, imprisoned, and banned from active participation in Turkish political life.

A group of dissidents from the ruling RPP established the Democratic Party in 1946. The Democrats were willing to ease secularism and state control of the economy, emphasizing the interests of peasants and large landowners. They won the 1950 and 1954 general elections, but government policies resulted in inflation, shortages, and worsening economic conditions. Prime Minister Adnan Menderes formed an investigation commission that recommended that if the RPP did not cease its "destructive criticism" of the government, the party should be banned from political life.[3]

Before any action could be taken, a group of military officers staged a coup in May 1960. The leaders of the DP were tried by a mixed civilian-military tribunal under the watchful eye of the military. This court sentenced Menderes, Minister of Foreign Affairs Zorlu, and Minister of Finance Polatkan to death. Despite these executions, the 1961 constitution extended freedom of association, press, publication, collective bargaining, and the right to strike, and provided social security for workers. Checks on executive power were ensured by the newly established Council of State, the Constitutional Court, and the Supreme Court of Appeals.

Political Climate: 1960-1971

From 1961 to 1965, Turkey was ruled by four different coalition governments headed by the RPP leader, İnönü. In the 1965 and 1969 general elections, the Justice Party (JP), established as the DP's replacement, won the majority of the popular vote.

Leftist intellectuals had established the Turkish Labor Party (TLP) in 1961. It never received more than 3 percent of the popular vote. The party's program advocated socialism through parliamentary democracy, but also stated that it was the party of the working class. The Turkish constitution prohibited associations based on class distinction and, although the constitutional question went unchallenged until 1971, the party's mere existence was enough to arouse the latent fear of communism. In 1963, a JP member founded the Turkish Association to Combat Communism.

The 1960s, however, saw an upsurge in political interest and activity by liberal intellectuals, leftists, and the majority of the university students. Their early slogans were for social justice, land reform, a more equitable distribution of income, and nonalignment. Anti-American sentiment was another factor that fostered radicalism among the youth. When the leader of the TLP made public the contents of 1963 secret bilateral agreements between Turkey and the United States, the government was obliged to renegotiate them because some clauses were incompatible with Turkish sovereignty. These issues corresponded to President Richard Nixon's demand for the total eradication of all hashish cultivation in Turkey. Although the government agreed to limit the growth of hashish at a significant cost to farmers, it did not satisfy the Americans. In retaliation, economic aid from the United States to Turkey decreased considerably, and credits were curtailed. Turkey became the only ally of the United States to have lost its most favored nation status. Thus, Turkish public opinion came to regard Turkey as being treated as a client state of the United States and not an ally. Demands were for Turkey's withdrawal from the North Atlantic Treaty Organization (NATO).

Strikes, boycotts, and demonstrations paralleled economic problems. Consequently, the radical Left and the main opposition party, the RPP, focused on an anti-government campaign. On March 12, 1971, the military issued a communiqué accusing the government of having led the country into anarchy, fratricidal strife, and social and economic unrest. The government resigned.

By 1970, the climate was set for political warfare. The adoption of a left-of-center position by the main opposition, the RPP, was not enough to satisfy the radical Left, which mocked social democracy as revisionism. Even the Turkish Labor Party's brand of socialism in the 1970s, which was deemed quite radical by the conservatives, would not appease the young militants. Extreme rightists seized a monopoly of nationalism. The Nationalist Action Party, under the leadership of ex-Colonel Türkeş, embodied ultra-nationalism, racism, irredentism, and national socialism.

The Rise of the Turkish Left

Between 1960 and 1970, there were only isolated acts of terrorism, in which leftists and rightists killed each other. These cases, however, were harbingers of nationwide terrorism in the years that followed.

In the 1960s, the journal *Yön* (Direction) symbolized a far more revolutionary kind of socialism from that of the Turkish Labor Party. By 1963, followers of *Yön* were elected as leaders of the debate club at Ankara University's political science faculty, which they used as a political base. In 1965, political science students who sold a socialist pamphlet in Ankara were attacked by religious youths. The press reported that the police had beaten the victims and had done nothing about the assailants.[4] During the 1965-1966 academic year, the debate clubs in various Turkish universities formed a national confederation.

On April 19, 1966, U.S. Secretary of State Dean Rusk arrived in Turkey to attend the Central Treaty Organization (CENTO) meetings. The debate club held a protest meeting announcing that NATO and CENTO opposed the principles of Turkish independence. When the leftist Türk-İş Trade Union organized a protest demonstration on behalf of Turkish workers on U.S. bases, for the first time, students and workers shouted anti-American slogans on the streets. The government took many demonstrators into custody and arrested some.

Leftist students viewed the JP government of Süleyman Demirel as supporting the "monopolist bourgeoisie," which collaborated with "U.S. imperialism" and subordinated the Turkish economy to it. Hence, it was impossible to develop heavy industry and become self-sufficient. Many of these students supported the TLP. When the rightists staged demonstrations in 1966 and 1968 to "condemn communism," leftists reacted with demonstrations to "condemn the United States" and were again attacked by rightist militants. Meanwhile, members of the Association to Combat Communism raided the TLP's national convention and also attacked and beat leftist students.

The security forces faced an unprecedented challenge. In 1965, there were approximately 30,000 policemen in Turkey trained to handle common crime. Their traditional orientation was to believe that communism was tantamount to treason. Thus, it was inevitable that leftist students would become targets of repression and that "help" from the Right would be welcomed. The government tried to keep demonstrations under control by forming a special team, hastily trained to handle mass movements.

Both leftists and rightists were increasingly active on campuses. A law, passed in 1967, raised the status of religious schools, allowing graduates to enter universities. The religious conservative element was thus introduced into higher education. Whether the state was trying to neutralize leftist militancy in the universities as leftists argued is debatable, but Atatürk's principle of a unified, secular education based on science was undone. Moreover, conservative leaders intensified their efforts to introduce religious norms into education.

Orthodox Islamic philosophy does not acknowledge a separation of religion and state; yet, under the republic, religion had been relegated to the personal sphere. This dichotomy allowed opportunistic politicians to blame the economic and social ills of the country on the deviations from traditional religious practice. By 1970, a former engineering professor, Necmettin Erbakan, established the National Order Party (NOP), which claimed to represent the interests of the Muslims and rejected Turkey's Western orientation. A revival of religious brotherhoods followed.

The Turkish youth movement was one of many around the world in the 1960s. Although Western democracies generally dealt with them within the confines of law, the Turkish state failed to do so. The reason may be twofold. First, the government intelligence and security forces chose to rely on rightist militants to handle leftist agitation on campuses and the streets. Second, the leftists had become so militant by the end of the 1960s that there was little room left for compromise.

Every month brought some new escalation. On July 15, 1968, the U.S. Sixth Fleet visited Istanbul. Leftist students protested, and when police tried to suppress the outburst, a student was killed. That same year, a controversial U.S. ambassador, Robert Komer—known to the Left as the "butcher of Vietnam"—was assigned to Turkey. When Komer visited the Middle East Technical University in Ankara in January 1969, leftist students on campus burned his limousine.

By 1969, mass movements had ceased, and terrorist acts had begun. Leftist militants sincerely came to believe that Turkey was ripe for a socialist revolution. Rightist commandos mobilized to fight them. On February 16, 1969, leftists held a demonstration, "the Mustafa Kemal march against imperialism." The same day, the *Bugün* newspaper called the Islamic faithful to a mass prayer and cautioned the public that guns might explode. Explode they did: A group of fanatic militants attacked the demonstrators, killing 2 people and wounding 104.

Meanwhile, some leftist militants were training in the camps of the PLO's al-Fatah group in Jordan. Others were trained by Kurdish rebels in Iraq. In June 1972, 14 armed terrorists were caught by the martial law command after they had infiltrated into Turkey on a boat that belonged to al-Fatah and had begun rural and urban guerrilla warfare. In 1973, a Turk was captured during an Israeli attack on a frogman training site in Lebanon. Approximately 400 Turkish militants had gone to the Palestinian camps alone. In May 1971, the Turkish People's Liberation Army/Front (TPLA-F) kidnapped and murdered the Israeli consul general of Istanbul, Ephraim Elrom. The TLPA-F defendants argued that their purpose was to demonstrate solidarity with the Palestinians and to pay them back for having trained the Turkish guerrillas. Rumor had it that Elrom had been murdered for having passed on to the Turkish security forces some names of the Turkish terrorists trained in Palestinian camps.

The Federation of Debate Clubs was reorganized as the Revolutionary Youth Federation (*Dev-Genç*) under radical leadership.[5] Out of *Dev-Genç* grew a large number of groups, such as the Turkish Revolutionary Workers' and Peasants' Party, the TPLA-F, and the Revolutionary Culture Hearths of the East.

The only difference among these groups was that of strategy, otherwise they followed the Marxist-Leninist or Maoist line. One theoretician of *Dev-Genç*, Dr. Hikmet Kıvılcımlı, advocated a socialist junta. According to him, the military should take over and bring a socialist cadre to power. Then, the revolution would forcibly be made under the protection of the military.[6]

In contrast, the Turkish People's Liberation Army's strategy was to begin revolution in the countryside, which they believed would spark further revolution in urban centers. To finance their revolution, TPLA members kidnapped people for ransom. The TPLA infiltrated the military and recruited some junior officers who were assigned to command workers', peasants', and youth regiments when the revolution began.[7]

The TPLA and TPLA-F drew inspiration both from Carlos Marighella's urban guerrilla tactics and Che Guevara's idea of simultaneous revolution in several neighboring countries. TPLA-F's revolutionary strategy was drawn by one of its leaders, Mahir Çayan, in his "Permanent Revolution I-II-III," which borrowed heavily from the Maoist concept of a people's war. Their goal was to "Vietnamize" Turkey. Accordingly, if southeastern Turkey could be declared a liberated zone, supportive foreign countries would be invited to join the struggle. In the northwest, TPLA and TPLA-F sought to carry out similar strategies. TPLA divided Turkey into zones, leaving the east and northeast to a simultaneous Kurdish nationalist insurrection. But the TPLA leaders, who had taken four U.S. servicemen hostage to collect ransom, robbed banks, and finally engaged in a shoot-out in the countryside with the gendarmerie, were arrested, tried in a military tribunal, and hanged.

These groups were alleged to have maintained relations with Soviet bloc diplomats. Russian and Czech-made arms and ammunition confiscated by the police pointed to Bulgaria as the conduit through which these arms were smuggled.[8] Other indicators of such connections were radicals' links to the Soviet cultural attaché, the Bulgarian vice consul, and confiscated materials printed in the Soviet Union. Furthermore, leaders of the Turkish Revolutionary Workers' and Peasants' Party would openly declare during their trial that one of their principles was to maintain ties with the East German, Chinese, and Albanian Communist Parties, as well as seeking financial aid from them. Their militants in Europe were active mainly in France and West Germany. The old Turkish Communist Party in Europe was already based in East Germany and had long been broadcasting to Turkey via the clandestine "Our Radio." Leftist militants visiting Europe and the Middle East lacked neither accommodation nor financing.

In March 1972, the Popular Front for the Liberation of Palestine held a meeting with the representatives of the Irish Republican Army (IRA), two Iranian groups, the Mujahedeen and Fedayeen, the Baader-Meinhoff gang, and the Turkish People's Liberation Army.

Turkish diplomacy, however, required that Turkey overlook the fact that Turkish terrorists were being trained in Libya and Iraq, in addition to Syria and Jordan. In 1974, Turkish military intervention in Cyprus resulted in a U.S. arms embargo to Turkey. Having lost Western political backing, Turkey strengthened its ties with the Arab world. It recognized the PLO and signed economic agreements with Libya, Iraq, and Saudi Arabia.[9]

But at home, the regime abolished the TLP and tried its leaders on charges of inciting a proletarian revolution.[10] In 1972, all types of student organizations were banned. The leaders of the first wave of terrorism were either captured and executed or died fighting the security forces.

By 1974, members of the TPLA and TPLA-F, who were set free in a general amnesty, had created a second generation of groups: the Revolutionary Path (*Dev-Yol*) and Revolutionary Left (*Dev-Sol*) groups, in addition to the Marxist-Leninist Armed Propaganda Unit. Terrorism was back in full force by 1975. The most dramatic difference between the first and second wave was the growing number of people involved in terrorist violence. Between 1975 and 1980, an estimated 30,000 terrorists operated in Turkey.[11] The Revolutionary Path established a "liberated zone" in northeast Anatolia, in the Fatsa township, and claimed to be a rival authority against the central government between 1978 and 1980. While Turkey embarked on a path toward civil war, leftist terrorist organizations enjoyed well-seasoned leadership from those released from jail.

Abuse of Power

The state apparatus had difficulty in coping with terror from both the Right and Left. One reason seems to have been the constitutional inadequacy in imposing a system of checks and balances on the major government institutions. Personal relations among the National Security Council, the National Intelligence Agency, the General Staff, and other government institutions set the pace for the flow of information (or the lack thereof). The chief officers of these groups felt free to withhold information from prime ministers. Further, the capricious preferences they displayed to collaborate with political factions helped stunt the growth of democracy.

Another reason the state was unable to control violence was that the two major political parties—the conservative Justice Party and the social democratic Republican People's Party—chose to ride tigers that proved to be uncontrollable. These tigers were the religiously oriented National Order Party and the neo-Nazi National Action Party (NAP). Coalition governments that included these two small parties permitted state agencies to be parceled out to extremist adherents of NOP and NAP ideology.

In the 1970s, the involvement of the counterinsurgency force in domestic affairs introduced official terrorism to Turkey. However, at no time could this have been interpreted as state terrorism, as can be seen in parts of South America. The issue also implicated the Americans, although the linkage was only made circumstantially. The Special War Office, formed under the auspices of the Joint United States Military Mission for Aid to Turkey (JUSMMAT) in Ankara, trained a special contingency team to be used in case of insurgency, civil war, or foreign occupation.

In 1971, the Istanbul Martial Law Commander General Türün used this force to interrogate suspected terrorists and revolutionaries in connection with a trumped-up charge against the incumbent Air Force Commander Batur, Navy Commander Kayacan and Army Commander Gürler. Türün used torture in trying to draw confessions from the accused—84 people including a general, a retired major, a geologist, a psychiatrist, and a well-known journalist. He believed that the generals and admiral in question had formed a leftist junta and were preparing a takeover.[12]

It is conceivable that Türün wanted to become chief of the General Staff and tried to eliminate commanders he saw as potential rivals. Further, there was indeed a leftist junta conspiracy among middle-ranking officers at that time. However, by misusing the counterinsurgency team, Türün not only damaged its reputation, but also fueled leftist accusations of U.S. interference in Turkish domestic affairs.[13] Gürler was promoted to chief of the General Staff, but resigned six months later.

On three other accounts, the credibility of the counterinsurgency force and the National Intelligence Agency came to be questioned publicly. On November 27, 1970, the Atatürk Cultural Center in Istanbul was destroyed by fire. In March 1972, the SS *Marmara* was sunk, and, in June 1972, the SS *Eminönü* was half-sunk. A General Staff briefing announced that all of the saboteurs were caught, that the same people were responsible for each of these acts, and that the court was "under the impression" that 1,165,000 Turkish lira (TL) had been paid to the militants from the Turkish Communist Party abroad. Yet, the accused were later released for lack of evidence. Whether the three incidents were acts of official terror calculated to level further blame against the Left or whether they were genuinely acts of leftist sabotage remains unclear to this day.

The "above-party" governments formed after the 1971 coup could not uphold the principle of law when faced with independent acts by the National Intelligence Agency, the counterinsurgency force, and factionalism among the military commanders. A close look at three important agencies shows how anarchy at the state level could occur under a system designed to regulate the roles of civilian authority, the military, and the intelligence community.

National Security Council

The National Security Council was established in 1961 as a measure against political parties that might abuse power. It was composed of the president, the prime minister, other major ministers, and military commanders. The National Security Council failed, however, to become the medium for military-civilian dialogue that was its original mission. The civilians considered the council to be a mechanism through which the military was able to intervene in politics. The military, on the other hand, regarded its duty to be the protection of the state's independence, unity, and peace and security. Under these strained circumstances, there failed to be an effective collaboration between civilians and the military in combating terrorism of any kind.

General Staff

According to the Turkish constitution, the cabinet recommends to the president a four-star general or an admiral for a four-year term as chief of the General Staff. Although the job was entirely a military concern, it was drawn into domestic affairs through representation on the National Security Council. Moreover, the chief of the General Staff always had the opportunity to become president. Turkey has had only two civilian presidents (Celâl Bayar, 1950-1960, and Turgut Özal, 1989-). The remaining six presidents came from the military, and half of those had once been chiefs of the General Staff. Therefore, it is likely that ambitious generals would view the post of chief as a step toward the presidency. This may explain some of the factionalism among generals. And such ambition may well have taken the course of using official terror against potential rivals by exploiting leftist terrorism.

National Intelligence Agency

The National Intelligence Agency (NIA) became a legal entity in Turkey only in 1965. The agency is under the office of the prime minister and has the duty of gathering intelligence on both internal and foreign affairs. The NIA frequently employs military personnel with the approval of the minister of defense and the chief of the General Staff. A certain peculiarity lies in the practice of employing military personnel in an agency that is also responsible for domestic intelligence.

The law regarding the NIA is nebulous in designating to whom the secretary general of the agency reports. In practice, this individual has felt free to present reports to whichever echelon he deemed appropriate, without having to go through the prime minister. In addition, the NIA secretary general has traditionally, with few exceptions, been part of the military. The system has thus been conducive to illegal acts, the least of which has been to use agents provocateurs in the universities without the knowledge or approval of the chief executive.

In the past, the NIA's coordination with the security forces was minimal. The lack of coordination and mutual respect between the civilians and military authorities made Turkey an ideal playground for terrorists, including those within the state apparatus.

Official terrorism continued well into the late 1970s, as the economic crisis deepened and international financial institutions refused to extend credit to Turkey unless political stability was achieved. Within a single three-month period in 1977, 89 leftists and 17 rightists were murdered. On May 1, 1977, DISK (The Revolutionary Workers' Union) held a huge demonstration in Istanbul's Taksim Square. Gunmen opened fire onto the crowd from the Intercontinental Hotel and the Water Administration Building that faced the square. During the ensuing panic, light armored police cars attacked the demonstrators, and 35 people were killed. In 1987, a former deputy prime minister told the press that the counterinsurgency force had been responsible for the shootings. This admission implicated the chief of the General Staff.

On June 2, 1978, Prime Minister Süleyman Demirel sent a secret personal letter to the opposition leader, Bülent Ecevit, warning him that there was reason to believe that an assassin was going to shoot Ecevit from a Sheraton Hotel window with a high-powered telescopic rifle during an RPP election rally scheduled the next day in Taksim Square. Ecevit released this letter to the press. The commander of the Turkish army "voluntarily" retired the same day. Simultaneously, 200 counterinsurgency officers were taken into custody. The general implicated in this act of official terror retired peacefully, while the younger officers were punished and expelled from the force. Some of these unemployed professional fighters might have become mercenaries for various terrorist organizations—a side effect of official terrorism.

The Rise of Rightist Terrorism

By 1968, commando camps were established by the Nationalist Action Party to train young men through military discipline to combat communism.[14] The trainers were retired officers. In 1968 alone, about 1,000 men underwent commando training and education by "nationalist" writers and teachers. It was not difficult to find recruits from among shantytown dwellers whose youth remained largely uneducated, unskilled, and unemployed. Through this training, these young men were given a purpose and good pay, as well as satisfying their machismo. These camps were known to the state. When the RPP argued that the camps were illegal, unconstitutional, and against party laws, Türkeş defied the opposition and won the day. The government remained silent.

Throughout 1970, violence continued in the universities, as well as during labor demonstrations and strikes. None of the rightist commandos responsible for the murders of leftist students or for bombing the homes of liberal, democratic-minded professors were apprehended. The Idealist Youth Associations (the Grey Wolves), the militant organ of the NAP, became bolder. In December 1970, they announced that any government action against them would bring a nationwide retaliation against police chiefs. Besides extorting money from businesses, the Grey Wolves gained ideological support, as well as voluntary financial contributions from middle-class people who were extremely wary of the radical Left. The Idealists did not have a clear-cut ideology, but they followed Türkeş'

"Nine Lights," which was based on ultra-nationalism, collectivism, anti-communism, and extreme statism.

Having established rival student organizations, militants from the Right and Left began to "occupy" student hostels, high schools, and university campuses. NAP's propaganda arm included 15 newspapers and 23 journals.[15] Even the police were divided into factions: POL-BİR aligned with the NAP line and POL-DER with a leftist orientation, a situation that had a disastrous effect on the country, as well as ensuring the security forces' loss of credibility.

At the same time, 10 militant religious groups existed. These included the Islamic Liberation Army, the Turkish-Islamic Liberation Union, the Turkish-Islamic Liberation Front, the Universal Brotherhood Front, Suicide Corps of the Shari'a, and the Turkish Revolutionary Shari'a Army.[16] These groups did not identify with the Islamic revolution in Iran, though one cannot discount ties between Turkish religious militants and their Iranian counterparts in Europe. It is not known whether these groups had links with the National Order Party.

Two months after the 1971 coup, the NOP was abolished on grounds that its aim was to render Turkey a theocracy. But within two years, that party was to appear under a new name, the National Salvation Party (NSP), without any challenge from the authorities who banned it in the first place. By law, any political leader whose party is closed by an order of the Constitutional Court was not to be a candidate for political office for at least five years. Not a single public or military prosecutor, however, reacted to Erbakan's candidacy or to his assumption of the NSP leadership.[17] Neither a state of law nor the law of the state functioned. Later, it was revealed that then-Air Force Commander Batur had made a deal with Erbakan and brought him back to Turkey from his self-imposed exile in Switzerland.[18]

The Nationalist Action Party leadership was also brought to trial, but the party was not abolished. Although Türkeş was taken into custody and tried, he managed to evade all accusations because they were based on circumstantial evidence. If the pattern with Erbakan holds, then there is a question of who made a deal with Türkeş and on what terms. Clearly, the "nationalist" commandos were considered pillars of the state until the 1980 coup.

After 1971, all the associations were abolished, but the Idealists continued to function within NAP's youth branch. Before the leftists had the chance to reorganize, the Idealist commandos began armed assaults in March 1974. They raided the largest student hostel in Istanbul, wounding 24 students and murdering 4 workers, as well as raiding the Middle East Technical University campus and hostels and the Hacettepe University in Ankara, using guns and dynamite. In January 1975, the Idealists attacked students at the Istanbul Technical University. The police allegedly remained passive. Throughout 1975, murders, attacks, and armed raids on campuses and high schools and at RPP offices continued on a larger scale in 23 provinces. Student boycotts in universities were broken by Idealist attacks.

Meanwhile, Nationalist Action Party parliamentarians pressed for personnel changes in state agencies, universities, and schools. They placed their own followers in top and middle management positions and acted as an employment and student placement agency for unqualified Idealist youth. The NAP infiltrated the security forces, which explains why their commandos often went unapprehended or, when caught, were released.

In 1974, Ecevit's minister of the interior attempted to reorganize the security forces by introducing new personnel. Shortly afterward, he was forced to resign because of an illicit affair, which was rumored to have been a setup. Nonetheless, the state permitted the police cadres and the Ministries of Labor and Education to be parceled out to NAP followers. State Economic Enterprises, directorships of teachers' colleges and lycées were filled with NAP ideologues.

In 1975, violence spread to the shantytowns. Commandos tried to occupy high schools in those neighborhoods. Gunshots and automatic rifle fire became commonplace during street fights. In 1979, a repentant Idealist, a 19-year-old shantytown dweller, exposed their modus operandi to the press. The more experienced Idealists taught the young recruits how to shoot and handle explosives. They were assigned to extort money from businessmen. Furthermore, if any Idealist attempted to leave the organization, the commandos would torture and kill him.[19] After the young man's confession was revealed, the newspaper *Hergün*, an organ of the NAP, announced that the confessor was a Communist Chinese agent, an agent provocateur who had incited the Idealists to use violence.

By 1977, the minister of the interior alerted the cabinet about the potential of increased violence perpetrated by commando hit teams. Demirel was adamant: He would not admit that the rightists committed crimes. The commandos paid no heed to the prime minister's public gesture of goodwill. Demirel was riding too wild a tiger. Terrorism had now begun to target university professors. Homes were bombed, some faculty members were assaulted, and an associate professor was killed in Erzurum. In December 1977, a group of workers, recently hired at the Middle East Technical University campus in Ankara, attacked a student forum with bombs and gunfire, leaving 1 student dead and 23 wounded.

In December 1978, the eastern city of Kahramanmaraş lived through a five-day-long pillage of Alawi-owned businesses and the murders of 111 Alawi citizens. A total of 803 people were brought to trial because of this incident. It was established that several of the defendants were Idealist militants. Furthermore, the attackers had shouted NAP slogans and carried the party emblem. That the homes and businesses of NAP members were spared pointed to an organized and well-planned operation. Somehow, the court failed to establish an official link between these terrorists and the NAP, but as a result of the Kahramanmaraş massacre, the government declared martial law in 13 provinces.

In February 1979, Abdi İpekçi, a renowned journalist and editor of the daily *Milliyet*, was murdered in Istanbul. The murderer was the Idealist militant Mehmet Ali Ağca, who later earned an international reputation for trying to assassinate the Pope. Ağca escaped from a high-security prison while his trial was going on. Those who helped him escape were never found. Likewise, the murderers of five professors and the assailants of two more were unaccounted for. Some disappeared without a trace or fled abroad. One was caught for other crimes and confessed to having been involved in the killing of one faculty member that was ordered by high NAP circles. At court, he changed his confession and claimed that this information was extracted from him under torture. In another case, West Germany refused to return the alleged murderer of another professor because the Turkish authorities could not guarantee that the man would not be given the death penalty if found guilty.

Many "nationalist" commandos who were given prison sentences went through a transformation: They merged their ideology with militant Islam. Another right-wing terrorist organization of the 1970s was the Raiders Association, the youth organ of the National Salvation Party. The Raiders' ideology centered around an Islamic revolution and rejected nationalism and democracy as alien doctrines for Muslims. Despite being a right-wing group, it generally clashed with the Idealist militants and, in some areas, cooperated with left-wing organizations against the Idealists.[20]

After the 1980 coup, many Idealist militants opted to embrace Islam in jail, where they served time along with the Raiders. Religious literature was abundant in jails, as opposed to limited secular literature, thus encouraging the widespread "conversion" of the formerly "pagan" Idealists. By 1988, Türkeş was to openly throw his lot with the Islamic fundamentalists.

Political Climate: 1971-1985

Government efforts to pass reform legislation were hampered by party strife. The 1961 constitution was amended at the request of the government to limit freedoms enjoyed by universities, the press, radio and television, and labor unions and associations. Moreover, an amendment gave the government the power to legislate by decree, which strengthened executive power. But it was impossible to have a strong government in Turkey unless the election law was amended to prevent the need for support from extremist parties. This did not happen. Furthermore, between 1960 and 1972, the state had granted general and partial amnesty nine different times, partly to appease the small rightist parties. Amnesty was thought of as a preventive measure because depenalization would theoretically result in decriminalization. However, repeat offenses made a mockery of rehabilitation.

For example, when general elections were held in October 1973, the National Salvation Party gained 38 seats in the parliament and 3 seats in the senate. Turkey was to be ruled by a caretaker government because the parties could not agree to a coalition scheme. In January 1974, however, an RPP-NSP coalition was formed. These strange bedfellows remained in government for nine months. Meanwhile, Ecevit granted a general amnesty, and political criminals were set free.

In April 1975, it was the turn of JP leader Demirel to form a coalition with Erbakan (NSP) as deputy prime minister and Türkeş (NAP) as second deputy. Türkeş's deputy premiership gave the NAP a say in the country's affairs far beyond its parliamentary strength or popular support. The only factor that brought these right-wing parties together was their common opposition to Ecevit. Otherwise, their doctrines ranged from liberal-conservative to neo-Nazi.

When Demirel's coalition finally had to resign, Ecevit then formed a coalition government with two more moderate parties in 1978, providing some new hope. As a first measure, the government formed a special committee to combat terrorism. One of its major tasks was to enforce a strict check on firearms and licenses. In the past, provincial governors had issued more gun licenses than was warranted. In addition to smuggled arms, there were illegal factories in the Black Sea region that produced large numbers of copies of foreign-made guns. The second task was to reorganize student hostels that had become safehouses for armed militants. Analysts agreed that Ecevit's success depended on his government's ability to remain free from terrorists' influence. Ecevit tried to prove his treatment of terrorists was evenhanded, so much so that a number of leftist activists were quite disappointed. Previous governments had failed because they discriminated between militants. "One heavily armed group was considered the defender of the Republic, the other was branded as traitor."[21]

During a debate on the 1978 fiscal year budget in the House-Senate Committee, it was alleged that the counterinsurgency department played one student camp against the other through provocation, infiltration, and acts of sabotage. Ecevit promised to reorient the counterinsurgency force, but could not secure the cooperation of the military.[22] To curb student violence, the government issued identification cards to student hostel residents, appointed new directors to the hostels, and set up police substations in hostels staffed by uniformed and plainclothes police officers.

But by March 1978, the death rate in civil strife was on the rise. Türkeş had lost control of his Idealists. Leftist militants were not happy with a social democrat like Ecevit, either. A struggle against a respected left-wing leader like Ecevit had less emotional appeal to workers and students. Moreover, Ecevit's desire to legalize the Turkish Communist Party might expose the Left's electoral weakness. A right-wing Nationalist Front government or even a military junta would have been more suitable for leftist militants.

A bomb attack on the Istanbul University campus killed six students. People from the legal, military, and intelligence establishments were murdered. A military judge involved in the detection and trial of extreme leftists was killed in a mysterious car crash. Ankara's chief public prosecutor, investigating the illegal activities of right-wing radicals, also was gunned down.

In September, 9 people were killed and more than 100 others wounded in what looked like a sectarian clash between Sunnis and Alawis in Sivas. The government reacted by deploying 20,000 gendarmes in cities throughout Turkey. Expert technical advice on antiterrorism was solicited from Scotland Yard. The government indicated that it would disband the right-wing and left-wing police associations, but failed to do so. In November, radical elements in the RPP blocked the passage of an antiterrorism bill that would have increased the law enforcement power of local officials, the police authority to search premises and arrest suspects, and the court's power to expedite the judicial process when terrorist acts were involved. The administrative system was not adjusted to cope with terrorism. The police complained that the military and civilian judges released some terrorists, but their own reports did not contain adequate evidence.[23]

Shortages, protest demonstrations, strikes, and murder continued. By the summer of 1979, the military began to display an interventionist approach. Ultra-conservative factions in the military were ready for a coup to "cleanse the country of Communists." Terrorism continued with full force despite martial law: During Ecevit's term in office, 1,172 people were murdered.

In the October 1979 by-elections, the RPP lost votes and again Demirel formed a new coalition cabinet whose program included the revival of state security courts, a ban on all politically oriented associations, and a request for emergency powers. The RPP opposition blocked this legislation; only the leftist police and teachers' associations were banned. The country had long suffered the damaging effects of "opposition for the sake of opposition." Even under rampant terrorist threats to the state, the civilian leadership failed to cooperate. Partisanship between and factionalism among the political parties outweighed common sense.

In January 1980, military commanders issued a letter of warning. Prime Minister Demirel was offended because his cabinet had just received a vote of confidence and was about to begin work. The National Assembly immediately began deliberations on the long-delayed package of antiterrorist legislation. Demirel later contended that the reason terrorism could not be prevented in spite of martial law was because the military had already decided there was to be a takeover.[24] This contention seems reasonable in that the terror stopped immediately after the September 12, 1980 coup. General Nevzat Bölügiray, the martial law commander of Adana, in his memoirs, states that the CGS had announced to the commanders in April 1980 that a coup was in the making.[25]

In July 1980, unidentified terrorists killed former Prime Minister Erim and an RPP deputy. Against presidential and public pleas for collaboration between the two major parties, the JP and RPP took turns intensifying opposition to each other. In May 1980, for example, Ecevit would not even agree to Demirel's offer for an early election. And Türkeş' NAP remained the principal power that kept Demirel's minority government in office. The NAP had practically become a state within a state. Although Demirel was fully aware of the NAP's role in political violence, he overlooked the issue in spite of the warnings of martial law commanders on the equal threat of right-wing and left-wing terror.

Moreover, both the NAP and NSP, as well as RPP, criticized martial law commanders who did not favor them. The commanders were beginning to sense that in the future they may be held accountable by either of those parties for not discriminating between terrorists.[26] The RPP and NSP held secret negotiations to topple Demirel's government. When they failed to reach an agreement, Demirel obtained a vote of confidence as a result of the RPP-NSP impasse. But the parliament failed to gain a quorum, thus failing to address the law-and order legislation. When Demirel and Ecevit met in late July 1980, Ecevit agreed to accept the establishment of state security courts and to grant a state of emergency power to the government, but refused Demirel's call for an early election. He maintained that it would be impossible to take voters to the polls without more bloodshed.

On September 6, 1980, Erbakan, the NSP mayor of Konya, and the Raiders Association staged a demonstration demanding the "redemption of Jerusalem." The Raiders went further, demanding a return to Islamic law and the closure of stores selling liquor and tobacco. They destroyed a beer house. The crowd prevented the playing of the national anthem and demanded recitation of passages from the Koran. This event was the last straw for the army.

Six days later, notification of a coup was broadcast over the radio at 4:00 a.m. Demirel, Ecevit, and Erbakan were taken from their Ankara residences and interned by the military. Türkeş went into hiding until convinced that his life was not in jeopardy. A decade later, the NAP trial was still in progress, and Türkeş once again managed to escape incarceration.

Terrorism ceased. Many militants escaped abroad and took advantage of political asylum granted by Western European countries, which disregarded their criminal background because of their political motivation. Accordingly, 2,871 separatist, 3,822 leftist, 235 rightist, and 23 religious militants, in addition to 2,437 militants of undetected persuasion, remain at large.[27]

The September Regime

During three years of military rule, mass arrests were made, and trials begun, some of which continued into the 1990s.[28] Between 1978 and 1980, 5,000 people had been murdered, and 12,000 were wounded in terrorist violence. A total of 822,632 arms of various types—including infantry and automatic rifles, submachine guns, mortars, and rocket launchers—were confiscated, along with 5,454,925 rounds of ammunition. Nearly 1,500 people were arrested and charged with arms smuggling. Of the 26 militants who received the death penalty, 21 were executed.

In 1981, the military regime closed down all political parties and banned their leaders from political activity. But, in the 1983 elections, President Kenen Evren's candidate for office lost to the civilian-led Motherland Party. Although the Turkish people had welcomed the September 12 coup because terrorism was eliminated, they did not want permanent military rule.

The coup, however, brought several major changes in the system. The 1982 constitution put a 10 percent electoral threshold, keeping minor parties out of parliament, the economy was liberalized, and the police force was reorganized. The entrance requirement to the coeducational police colleges was raised from an elementary to a high school education. In 1990, the security department boasted a 100,000-strong force, advanced forensic laboratories, and an absence of ideological orientation among its ranks.[29] The Confession Act of 1982 provided reduced sentences to terrorists who cooperated with the security forces.[30] Many liberal and leftist teachers, professors, and civil servants were purged, but in 1989, the infamous Law No. 1402 was revoked, and many of these people are being reinstated to their former positions. University administrations were brought under a coordinating body, the Council of Higher Education, to choose rectors and deans. New universities were built nationwide to provide local higher education.

Ironically, a major legacy of the September 12 coup was the increasing visibility of Islamic movements in Turkey. Fundamentalists no longer hide their goal of transforming the secular republic into an Islamic one. A culture of religion now exists with publications, subsidized student hostels, and the construction of mosques and religious schools. One patron saint of this movement was a brother of the former prime minister and current president. Through his connections in Saudi Arabia, he was instrumental in establishing the Faisal Finance and Al Baraka "Turk" private finance companies in Turkey.[31] Many Turks see this as Saudi subversion. Added to this are the activities of the Iranian-supported *Hezbollah* and Jordanian-based *Hizb' al Tahrir* groups, which try to export the Islamic revolution. In March 1990, 33 terrorists, including an Iranian citizen, were caught in Istanbul. They called themselves the "Commandos of Revenge of the Shari'a" and had been trained in the Iranian city of Qom.

The strategy of the Islamists is a patient one. Although the number of Turkish vocational schools has declined in the past 10 years, religious schools have increased. These schools now educate 231,654 students; in the past decade, 42,000 students from religious high schools graduated from universities and took professional positions.[32]

As a social phenomenon, the Islamic movement is acceptable, but turning Islamic values into a political approach is an altogether different matter. This approach has already generated violence. In 1984, a religious group murdered a student in Erzurum's Atatürk University for not fasting during Ramadan. The names of ultra-rightist religious groups revealed by security forces in 1989—the Revolutionary Islamic Youth, Islamic Revival, and the Islamic Salvation Army—do not point to peaceful motives.[33] In December 1989, one such group raided an art exhibition in Istanbul and destroyed paintings. Cases of young girls forced into Islamic groups and into wearing Islamic garb have been repeatedly cited in Turkish newspapers.

Terrorism in the 1990s

A champion of laicism and Atatürk, Professor Muammer Aksoy, was murdered in Ankara on February 1, 1990. Many events indicate that the fundamentalists may not remain peaceful much longer. In 1988, Türkeş declared at the party congress that he had shelved his traditional pan-Turkish policy in favor of a turn toward Islam. With the potential help of professional commandos, in addition to those trained in Iran, the fundamentalists may begin to engage in terrorism.[34]

Left-wing terrorists have also jumped onto the bandwagon of violence. On March 7, 1990, a much-respected journalist, Çetin Emeç of *Hürriyet*, was murdered. What he and the late Professor Aksoy had in common was a dedication to democracy and secularism. The Islamic commandos and Revolutionary Left simultaneously assumed responsibility for the murder.

The Turkish radical Left is also seeking a comeback. In January 1989, the Revolutionary Left group bombed the Economic Development Foundation offices, the Turkish-American Businessmen's Association, and the Metal Industrialists' Union. Currently, it is apparent that the outlawed revolutionary Left is trying to infiltrate the universities and once more take the lead in radicalism. This group led, if not initiated, student demonstrations protesting the presence of plainclothes and uniformed police officers on campus.

In the winter of 1988, top leaders of the Turkish left-wing organizations in Paris, London, and Munich held a meeting in which *Dev-Yol* and *Dev-Sol* agreed to create a Turkish Revolutionary Front to continue their struggle within Turkish territory. However, because illegal weapon sales have dramatically decreased in Turkey since 1980, surviving would be quite difficult even if some militants moved back to Turkey. Other groups also recruit in Europe.[35]

In March 1990, security and intelligence forces reported that 19 different Turkish left-wing organizations were located in Lebanon, Syria, Greece, Bulgaria, Greek Cyprus, France, Italy, Spain, Austria, Switzerland, Norway, Sweden, England, and East and West Germany.[36] Prospects for large-scale terrorism in Turkey remain limited. Nonetheless, left-wing and Islamic militants pose a potential threat, especially if they decide to collaborate.

Conclusion

Leftist and rightist ideological movements were catalysts for terrorism in Turkey during the 1970s. Left-wing activists opted for terrorism when they realized that leftist parties did not receive sufficient votes in Turkish elections to make any difference in Turkish politics. Moreover, youth movements worldwide and the theoreticians of the New Left—such as Debray, Che Guevera, and Carlos Marighella—left an indelible mark on

Turkish radicals. Ultra-rightist dogmas also weighed heavily on the dimensions that terrorism took.

In addition, superpower rivalry also had a political impact. Moscow tried to bring Turkey into its sphere of influence; the United States continuously pressured Turkey through economic and military sanctions.

The responsibility for mismanaging the crisis lay with the Turkish state because of its leaders' factionalism, cronyism, and the lack of trust between the military and civilians. Demirel argues that the civil state had become paralyzed since the 1960 coup. "The state," he said, "is a civilized institution; it survives on moral authority and not on force."[37] Accordingly, a civilian government that exists under the constant threat of a military takeover could hardly be expected to operate the state machinery effectively. The police force, the courts, and even martial law commanders feared that someday they would be held accountable for their actions by a military faction of an unknown persuasion. Demirel pointed out that when certain terrorists went scot-free, the state was unable to set an example to others.

Demirel stated that between 1965 and 1969, 80 percent of his time was devoted to trying to keep the military, students, and labor organizations under control. If the military, whose raison d'être is to protect the state against domestic and foreign enemies, rises against the state, one should not be surprised by anarchy on the streets. According to Demirel, terrorism is encouraged by such acts. In addition, he lamented that Turkish intellectuals did not respect the majority's will, that is, their choice of the JP as the ruling party. To Demirel, this meant that the elite looked down on the judgment of the so-called ignorant masses. And, thus, civilian government lacked the moral support of the society's most vociferous component.

Turkey's problems with terrorism are far from over. But today's society is now conscious of the institutional and community responsibility to combat terrorism. As much as terrorism and the ensuing coups damaged the respectability of the state, they also served a constructive purpose: An enlightened public opinion has emerged. Public accountability, human rights, freedom of thought and expression, and a national consensus against military coups has emerged. During those painful years, the Turkish public received basic lessons in democracy in the most difficult way possible. Perhaps the most important lesson was learning not to fear dissension. Whether the civilian politicians and military leaders have also learned these lessons, however, remains to be seen.

Glossary of Major Political Parties

The Republican People's Party (RPP)
Led by İsmet İnönü from 1938 to 1971
Led by Bülent Ecevit from 1971 to 1981
Closed down in 1981
Revived in 1983 as the Social Democratic Populist Party (SDPP)
Led by Professor Erdal İnönü
Splinter group formed the Democratic Left Party (DLP)
Led by Bülent Ecevit

The Democratic Party (DP)
Led by Celâl Bayar and Adnan Menderes from 1946 to 1960
Closed down in 1960
Revived in 1963 as the Justice Party (JP)
Led by Ret. Gen. Ragıp Gümüşpala and, as of 1965, by
  Süleyman Demirel
Closed down in 1981
Revived as the True Path Party (TPP) in 1983
Led by Süleyman Demirel

The National Order Party (NOP)
Led by Professor Necmettin Erbakan
Closed down in 1971
Revived as the National Salvation Party (NSP) in 1973
Led by Professor Necmettin Erbakan
Closed down in 1981
Revived as the Welfare Party (WP) in 1983
Led by Professor Necmettin Erbakan

The Nationalist Action Party (NAP)
Led by Alparslan Türkeş from 1965 to 1981
Closed down in 1981
Revived as the Nationalist Work Party (NWP) in 1983
Led by Alparslan Türkeş

The Motherland Party
Led by Turgut Özal from 1983 to 1989
Led by Yıldırım Akbulut since 1989

Notes

1. Lucille W. Pevsner, *Turkey's Political Crisis* (Westport, Conn.: Praeger Publishers, 1984), 6.

2. Uğur Mumcu, "40'ların Cadı Kazanı, *Cumhuriyet*, February 11-24, 1990; Alparslan Türkeş, *1944 Milliyetçilik Olayı*, 2nd ed. (Istanbul: Kutluğ Yayınları, 1972), 27-39.

3. Nusret Kirişcioğlu, *12 Mart, İnönü-Ecevit ve Tahkikat Encümeni Raporum* (Istanbul: Baha Matbaası, 1973).

4. Ali Yıldırım, *Belgelerle FKF, Dev-Genç* (Ankara: Yurt Yayınları, 1988), 25-34.

5. Yılmaz Çetiner, *El Fateh* (Istanbul: May Yayınları, 1970); George S. Harris, "The Left in Turkey," *Problems of Communism* 29, no. 4 (July-August 1980): 3.

6. Himet Kıvılcımlı, *Dev-Genç Seminerleri* (Istanbul: Kıvılcım Yayınları, 1989).

7. Sinan Doğan, *THKP-C; Doğuşu ve İlk Eylemleri*, 3rd ed. (Istanbul: Kaynak Yayınları, 1987).

8. Uğur Mumcu, *Silah Kaçakçılığı ve Terör*, 7th ed. (Istanbul: Tein Yayınları, 1983); Idem, *Papa, Mafya ve Ağca*, 2nd ed. (Istanbul: Tein Yayınları, 1984); Metin Tamkoç, "International Terrorism: The Russian Connection," in *International Terrorism and the Drug Connection*, Ankara University Symposium, April 17-18, 1984, pp. 49-69; Claire Sterling, *Terör Ağı* (Istanbul: Yüce Yayınları, 1981).

9. "Turkey Tightens Its Ties with Arabs," *Jerusalem Post*, February 16, 1975.

10. Republic of Turkey, Martial Law Command's Case Against the TLP, No. 1971/48, July 26, 1971.

11. This number includes those on the Right.

12. Talât Turhan, *Bomba Davası*, 2 vols., 2nd ed. (Istanbul: Zafer Matbaası, 1986).

13. Oğuzhan Müftüoğlu, ed. *1960'lardan 1980'e Türkiye Gerçeği* (Istanbul: Patika Yayıncılık, 1989), 137-145; Engin Höke, *1960'lardan 1980'e Gençlik ve Mücadelesi* (Istanbul: Simge Yayınevı, 1989), 75.

14. Jacob Landau, *Türkiye'de Sağ ve Sol*, 2nd ed. (Ankara: Turhan Kitabevi, 1979), 305-309; The Public Prosecutor's Case Against the Nationalist Action Party, no. 27, October 1971.

15. Otmar Oehring, *Die Türkei im Spannungsfeld extremer Ideologien (1973-1980)* (Berlin: Klaus Schwarz Verlag, 1984), 307. The party's associations included youth, public employees, workers, teachers, technical workers, small businessmen, economists, peasants, women, journalists, movie, art and culture, labor unions, lawyers, doctors, radio and television workers, and, perhaps most important, the police force.

16. Ibid., 311.

17. Sadık Albayrak, *Türk Siyasi Hayatında MSP Olayı* (Istanbul: Araştırma Yayınları, 1989), 80.

18. "Secularism vs. Fundamentalism," *Briefing no. 732* (April 23, 1989): 12-16.

19. *İtiraf* (Istanbul: Aydınlık Yayınları, 1980).

20. Atilla Yayla, "Terrorism in Turkey," *Ankara Üniversitesi Siyasal Bilgiler Fakültesi Dergisi*, no. 3/4 (July-December 1989): 259.

21. "Smart Moves by Türkeş to Woo the RPP—But Can He Succeed?" *Briefing*, no. 156 (January 18, 1978): 4.

22. "What Lies Behind the Campaign to Expose Illegal Activities?" *Briefing*, no. 158 (February 1, 1978): 16.

23. Nevzat Bölügiray, *Sokaktaki Asker* (Istanbul: Milliyet Yayınları, 1989), 200-201.

24. Mehmet Ali Birand, *The Generals' Coup in Turkey* (London: Brassey's Defence Publishers, 1987), 39.

25. Bölügiray, *Sokaktaki Asker*, 577-581.

26. Coşkun Kırca, "Evren," *Milliyet*, November 13, 1989; Birand, *The General's Coup*, 42.

27. Report from the Ministry of the Interior, General Directorate of Security to the Grand National Assembly, Ankara, March 2, 1988. Courtesy of Süleyman Demirel.

28. On June 6, 1990, the Istanbul Military Court of Appeal sanctioned the death penalty for 5 Marxist-Leninist Armed Propaganda Unit militants and revoked 17 death sentences.

29. However, an alarming report recently appeared that noted the police cadres are filled with Islamic fundamentalists. "Poliste İslamcı Kadrolaşma," *Nokta*, no. 23 (June 10, 1990): 16-22.

30. On June 7, 1990, a confessor from the Marxist-Leninist Armed Propaganda Unit was shot to death by three men who claimed to belong to the armed unit of the Revolutionary Left terrorist organization.

31. Uğur Mumcu, "Birader Vakıfları," *Cumhuriyet*, January 6, 1987.

32. Hıfzı Veldet Velidedeoğlu, "Şeriatçıların Stratejisi," *Cumhuriyet*, April 12, 1987.

33. "Üniversitelerde Sağ Örgütler Güç Kazanıyor," *Hürriyet*, October 1, 1989.

34. "The Nationalists' Convention: A Turning Point for the 'Ülkücüs,'" *Briefing* (November 28, 1988): 11-17.

35. "The Beat Goes On," *Briefing*, no. 678 (March 28, 1988): 4.

36. "18 Ülke Türkiye'de Terörü Destekliyor," *Hürriyet*, March 18, 1990.

37. Author interview with Süleyman Demirel, Ankara, January 1990.

7
The Origins of the PLO's Terrorism

Barry Rubin

Why did the Palestine Liberation Organization adopt terrorism as the main instrument in its struggle during the 1960s and 1970s and as one of the primary aspects of its strategy in the 1980s and 1990s? Although the answer has often been taken for granted, it is a source of significant and useful subject matter for study.

Between 1969 and 1985, PLO member groups committed about 8,000 acts of terrorism—mostly in Israel, but more than 435 abroad as well—and killed more than 650 Israelis (more than three-quarters of whom were civilians), and hundreds of others, as well as wounding thousands.[1]

The PLO's attitude toward terrorism was built on several premises. First, the PLO defined military action of any kind that furthered its cause as "armed struggle." In contrast, the PLO defined terrorism as a criminal, pointless act, although not, in the Western sense, as an attack on civilians. Thus, the purpose—rather than the target—was the key element in justifying or condemning an action. Over time, the PLO came to see the whole Western idea of terrorism as a plot to single out the PLO for condemnation. The difference between violence and terrorism, explained Yassir Arafat, was the difference "between legitimate armed resistance and wanton acts of destruction. We are opposed to terrorism because we are the victims of terrorism. Any armed resistance can be condemned as a terrorist activity." The problem, however, was that most of the PLO's armed struggle was planned and waged against civilians.[2]

Second, terrorism was made acceptable and attractive by the PLO's attitude toward Israel. The PLO's decision to wage attacks on Israeli civilians arises naturally from a view of Israel as a fragile, artificial entity and from the desire to destroy it totally. The Jews are considered to be cowards, whose natural status is dependency on Muslim rulers. The Arabs are superior fighters, at least if they use proper tactics. Israel is considered to be an artificial entity that, when pushed, would quickly collapse. The PLO Charter stated that all or most Israeli Jews have no political rights and should be driven from the land.

Finally, terrorism proved to be a "pragmatic" way to mobilize Palestinian and Arab support, raise the international priority of the Palestinian issue, intimidate opponents, and discourage Western countries from supporting Israel. In short, terrorism seemed a strategy that was easy, justifiable, and likely to be successful.

If not pushed into the sea, the Jews should be loaded onto boats. What the PLO would have actually done if it had succeeded is impossible to prove, but not difficult to imagine. The PLO considered itself at war with a society—not just an army or post-1967 occupation—and with the West, not just Israel. The struggle's aim "is not to impose our will on the enemy," explained the PLO's official magazine, "but to destroy him in order to take his place...not to subjugate the enemy but to destroy him."

Because all Israelis are, by definition, settlers in the illegal occupation of Palestine—and because all civilians could be said to be preserving and furthering the state's existence—they were again appropriate targets. "One fights the kind of war he can afford," said one PLO official. "There are not Israeli civilians—women and men, all are ready at any moment to use arms against us." On one hand, this view can be ascribed to Palestinian revolutionaries' incredible hatred and demonization of Israelis. On the other hand, it could be considered a rational analysis because the conquest and destruction of Israel entailed its people's destruction, demoralization, or departure.

Algeria's revolution formed the main model for the PLO, whose early cadre were often trained there. The Algerians seemed to have defeated France and expelled the French colonists largely by using terrorism. If an ideological justification was needed to reinforce this success, it could be found in the notion of Marxists and of the Algerian theorist Franz Fanon that violence restored the pride and identity of the colonized. Yet, this was a misreading of history. The French settlers were ruled by France's government and protected by its army. When the war became too expensive, the French government handed over the country to the Arabs, and the settlers could do nothing. Because the PLO erroneously saw Israel as a Western colony, the PLO believed that the use of international terrorism would lead the United States and its European allies to withdraw support, thus eventually causing the demise of Israel.

Another point in common between the Algerian and Palestinian revolutionaries was a fundamental structural split between those inside and those outside the country. The Algerians' "inside" leadership was largely destroyed by French counterinsurgency, but the "outside" army and government-in-exile survived to take over the country. The PLO, long unsuccessful in mass mobilization, also made "outside" forces the key factor. Even during the *intifada*, PLO leaders in Tunis gave little autonomy to "inside" forces, blocked development of an independent leadership, and planned to impose itself on the West Bank and Gaza in any Palestine state.

"The Israelis have one great fear, the fear of casualties," said Arafat, and this attitude has been a guiding principle in PLO thinking. If enough Israelis could be killed by Arab armies in war or by Palestinian terrorists, the PLO believed Israel would collapse or surrender. Thus, at a 1970 symposium, an al-Saiqa man noted that the Jews could not bear to live under so much tension and threat forever: "The Zionist efforts to transform them into a homogeneous, cohesive nation have failed." PLO leaders sincerely thought Zionism an imperialist plot that even Jews opposed. "We mean to exploit the contradictions within Israeli society," explained Arafat.

"Any objective study of the enemy will reveal that his potential for endurance, except where a brief engagement is concerned, is limited," concluded the Fourth Palestinian National Congress (PNC) in 1968. "The drain on this potential that can be brought about by a long drawn-out engagement will inevitably provide the opportunity for a decisive confrontation in which the entire Arab nation can take part and emerge victorious."

Arafat and al-Fatah saw the purpose of attacks as,

> To prevent immigration and encourage emigration. To prevent the stabilization of capital. To destroy tourism. To prevent immigrants becoming attached to the land. To weaken the Israeli economy and to divert the greater part of it to security requirements. To create and maintain an atmosphere of strain and anxiety that will force the Zionists to realize that it is impossible for them to live in Israel. The gradual achievement of the above objectives will inevitably bring about the disintegration of the enemy state and its eventual dissolution. This is why we insist upon a people's war of liberation, which alone can exhaust the enemy, destroy its stability and pave the way for a quick blow by the regular armies at the right moment.[8]

Even when the PLO lost faith in Arab armies, it thought anti-civilian terrorism could bring victory. The Israeli "will find himself isolated and defenseless against the Arab soldier in his house, on his land, on the road, in the cafe, in the movie theatre, in army camps and everywhere....These acts will force him to consider and compare the life of stability and repose that he enjoyed in his former country and the life of confusion and anxiety he finds in the land of Palestine. This is bound to motivate him towards reverse immigration."[9]

A dozen years later, internal PLO documents preached the same doctrine. The enemy's "greatest weakness is his small population. Therefore, operations must be launched which will liquidate immigration into Israel," attacking absorption centers, sabotaging water and electricity, "using weapons in terrifying ways against them where they live...attacking a tourist installation during the height of the tourist season."[10]

Over and over, PLO groups reiterated this message. For to agree that Israel would not eventually be eliminated would be to accept that Palestine would never be restored to the Arabs. Even those willing to undertake a compromise for the sake of peace in the 1990s still held firmly to the belief that there would be another stage in which, one way or another, Israel would disappear from the map.

Arafat spoke of "the conscious and calculated linking of armed struggle and political struggle" because the Palestinians "cannot possible achieve their objectives without military pressure on Israel."[11] In fact, this had the exact opposite effect: hardening Israel's resolve, making it unwilling to negotiate with the PLO.

Without quite realizing it, Abu Iyad, leader of the Black September international terrorist operation, explained what was wrong with the PLO terrorist strategy. The Israeli soldier, he claimed, "does not believe in this war except from the angle of self-defense. If we can by our behavior reach the heart of this man to convince him that in reality we are not, as the Zionists would have him believe, barbarians who want to kill him and throw his women and children into the sea, then it would be possible to separate psychologically between the man and the Zionist, between the Jewish soldier and the colonialist Zionist military institution." Yet, PLO actions throughout the years seemed to embody the "barbarian" theory; Abu Iyad himself suggested that the way to resolve the conflict was to persuade Arab states to take back all their Jewish nationals who had once emigrated to Israel.[12]

Third, al-Fatah usually—though not always—wanted to concentrate its military efforts against Israel directly; the Democratic Front for the Liberation of Palestine, the Popular Front for the Liberation of Palestine, and several smaller PLO groups were more interested in international attacks on those they saw as Western imperialists who supported Israel or Arab reactionaries who interfered with the Palestinian or regional revolution. Their targets were influenced by the demands and interests of their Arab state sponsors. The use of terrorism as political blackmail was also a good device for raising funds and ensuring support, particularly from the wealthy Arabs of the Persian Gulf.

Although al-Fatah became increasingly concerned about the damage done by international terrorism to its image and political prospects—thus using deniable fronts like Black September in the 1970s and Force-17 in the 1980s—smaller groups had a different perspective. They thought that bad publicity was the result of the West's failure to understand the Palestinian cause's justice. Still, even George Habash, one of the principal organizers of PLO terrorism, understood the way to counteract this was to plan "so carefully that they [the attacks] do not lead to third parties being harmed, and ensure that the damage they do is restricted to the enemy and his interests." In addition, "there must also be adequate and extensive information coverage to make it absolutely clear that right is entirely on our side in every operation we carry out."[13] But Habash—like Hawatmeh, Ahmad Jibril, Abu Nidal, Abu al-'Abbas, Abu Ibrahim, and other Palestinian revolutionaries in and out of the PLO—had a clear reason for international terrorism. "Our enemy is not Israel alone," explained Habash. "Our enemy is Israel, the Zionist movement, imperialism and the forces of reaction. It is thus natural that our military strategy should conform to our political definition of the enemy. These operations inflict material and moral injuries on the enemy, and at the same time greatly raise the morale of our people."[14]

Fourth, the PLO knew that terrorism was popular among the masses of Palestinians and Arabs. The very extremism of the remedy was itself taken as proof of the cause's justness. There were no significant moral compunctions, self-doubts, or self-criticism about the use of these means. Arab politicians or writers did not produce articles or speeches urging empathy for the victims or agonizing about the deliberate killing of women and children. Criticizing another PLO group or an operation carried political costs—accepting terrorism did not, at least within the Arab world. Those killed, even after committing the most brutal murders, became glorified martyrs; all the terrorists were popular heroes.

A similar assessment was made by Habash about a successful hijacking:

We realize that when the masses see a girl like Laila Khalid hijacking a plane and flying it over Lydda, and defying the enemy, they are proud and more determined than ever to fight, we believe that this is a genuine criterion for action, we believe that this kind of action is good for our cause, and we say: Certainly, world public opinion is quite important, and we shall try to make our position clear to it, we shall make every effort to increase our information activity. But even if world public opinion continues for a time to be unable to comprehend the considerations that lie behind these activities, we shall continue to engage in them, because our first criterion is the masses.[15]

In short, highly publicized terrorism was considered a key tool for winning mass support, and this factor was held to be more important than terrorism's negative effect on the West's perception of Palestinians and the PLO.

Some observers, however, doubted this tactic's effectiveness as a substitute for political organizing. A sympathetic Arab critic on the left commented, "Needless to say the Arab masses have become deeply habituated, since the rise of Nasirism, to respond to these kinds of spectacular stimuli [hijackings] on a purely emotional plane which rarely demands genuine sacrifices...does not even demand the slightest departure from the normal course of life so that the whole affair becomes a victory, by proxy, for the emotionally stirred masses."[16]

In short, terrorism became a spectator event, a "people's war" that avoided the need to involve the people. Yet, terrorism was also a stand-in for other achievements, an opiate of the Palestinian people for their continued suffering, lack of progress, and other Arabs' contempt. Thus, the publicity gained by Black September's attacks, under al-Fatah's orders, helped the guerrilla movement regain lost prestige after its 1970 disaster in Jordan.[17]

Terrorism had a similarly large but corrupting effect on the PLO's structure and leadership. Groups committed and escalated terrorism to increase their influence within the organization, to compete for power with the PLO, and to win sponsorship from Arab states. The PLO was never able to create a central command structure to coordinate or control the member groups, each of which had its own military apparatus. Thus, political discipline was impossible. Individual fighters would switch allegiances to a seemingly more active, effective chief. Arab regimes used terror against the PLO itself; Palestinian radicals murdered moderates.

International terrorism gained much attention for the PLO and Palestinian cause, but antagonized the West and did nothing to undermine Israel. Abu Jihad—architect of the massacre of Israeli athletes at the 1968 Munich Olympics, the 1975 seizure of the Savoy Hotel in Tel Aviv with 11 killed and 11 wounded, and the hijacking of an Israeli bus in 1978, with 33 killed and 82 wounded—and Abu Iyad, chief of the Black September group for international terrorism and assassination, became the two most powerful figures in the PLO next to Arafat. Moderates like Said Hammadi and 'Isam Sartawi were politically impotent, and, after their murder by Palestinian terrorists, Arafat left them forgotten and unavenged. The level of internal violence in the movement rose, and moderates were often the target. Arab states—mainly Syria, but also Iraq and Libya—assassinated PLO officials. Nablus mayor Zafir al-Masri was murdered by PFLP gunmen working with Syria. Yet, this deed did not damage the PFLP's status in the PLO.

Terrorism also had important commercial aspects. Abu Nidal and others were terrorists for hire. In Lebanon and elsewhere in the Middle East, the career of gunman made for high status and good pay, with perquisites that included the booty that resulted from looting local people and money from occasional involvement in drug smuggling. Precedent showed that those captured could well expect some new terrorist action or prisoner exchange might free them fairly quickly. The PLO recruited mercenaries who were not Palestinians or even Arabs.

As for ideology, terrorists were often far from fanatical. Former hostage Charles Glass discovered that his supposed Islamic fundamentalist captors talked about girls, rock music, and cars. "They were ordinary Lebanese teenagers with no commitment at all."[18] A romantic view of terrorism would have it that terrible oppression drives average people to commit horrendous acts. Still, even when other kinds of resistance are quite comprehensible, the leap to terrorism cannot be understood without considering the individuals' psychological factors, suspension of ethical constraints, and frustrated fantasies and neuroses.

By the 1980s, a PLO more interested in diplomatic solutions found it difficult to jettison the ideas or behavior that had become so deeply ingrained. Moreover, although PLO leaders sincerely expected armed struggle to weaken Israel, each such attack hardened the Israeli attitude against negotiating with the PLO or withdrawing from the occupied territories. Although the PLO was successful in reducing Western support for Israel, the use of terrorism aroused more sympathy for the Jewish state.

In short, active terrorism blocked the PLO's diplomatic option, while the memory of past attacks made compromise more difficult for both PLO leaders and their adversaries. Terrorism brought the PLO a great deal of helpful publicity among its Arab audience, while discrediting it in the eyes of the West. The focus on militarism and the downgrading of diplomacy ultimately gave the Arab regimes more, rather than less, leverage over the PLO. Egypt and Syria blocked PLO operations from their soil, and the PLO was expelled from Jordan and Lebanon.

This is not to say that terrorism was altogether counterproductive. It helped the PLO attain some objectives—acceptance by Arab regimes, hegemony among Palestinians, more international attention to resolving their issue—even while making it much harder to reach others. When the PFLP seized four airliners in 1970, the British magazine *The Economist* commented, "The great hijack worked. The hijackers have succeeded in making 'Palestinian' an international household word." In addition, European countries were successfully blackmailed into releasing terrorists they already held prisoner. Laila Khalid, for example, killed an Israeli security guard in a 1970 hijacking attempt, but was captured by other Israeli guards and turned over to British authorities when the plane landed in England. The British released her in exchange for the PFLP's hostages in Amman.[19]

Clearly, a major reason for the success and durability of Palestinian and PLO terrorism has been the help and protection of Arab states, which have provided money, safe haven, logistical help, training, weapons, secure rear areas, diplomatic backing, and protection against retaliation. The ability to obtain passports, ship arms and explosives via official diplomatic pouches, and obtain lavish financing has allowed terrorists to be far more prolific and deadly.

The PLO also joined a global network of guerrilla and terrorist groups and built valuable links to the Soviet Union and its East European satellites. It sent people to the Soviet bloc, China, and North Korea for training in guerrilla warfare that was often directly transferable to terrorist skills. Being able to do favors for radical governments and revolutionary groups also brought the PLO income and reciprocal favors. The first shipment of Soviet bloc military aid arrived through Syria in September 1972. Soviet-made antiaircraft surface-to-air missiles (SAM-7s) were found in Black September's arsenal in autumn 1973. In September 1973, the Czechs helped Black September to seize a train full of Soviet Jewish refugees traveling through their country to Austria. Moscow has also abetted terrorism in order to weaken U.S. influence, undermine Israel, and help its PLO ally.[20]

In Lebanon, the PLO trained more than 3,000 foreign terrorists from all over the world.[21] The PFLP worked closely with German, Italian, and Japanese groups, most notoriously with the Japanese Red Army's murder of 26 people and wounding of 80, mostly Puerto Rican pilgrims, at Israel's Lod Airport in May 1972. The PFLP cooperated with the German Baader-Meinhoff gang in several operations, including the 1976 hijacking ended by the Israeli rescue mission at Entebbe.

The PLO, of course, did not define its actions as terrorist, but rather as a people's guerrilla war by armed struggle. In fact, the PLO's inability to follow this course was a major reason for its emphasis on terrorism. After all, until the *intifada* began in 1987, the PLO neither mobilized the masses nor demonstrated success in guerrilla warfare. The original effort to strike from Jordan between 1967 and 1970 fizzled; the offensive from Lebanon between 1970 and 1982 consisted of sending small, suicide squads toward Israeli towns and villages.

The PLO's focus on terrorism, begun with its ideological orientation and aims, was heightened by its strategic refusal or inability to put the emphasis on political organizing or regular guerrilla warfare. The movement was unable—and relatively disinterested—in mobilizing the masses through political organization in the 1960s and 1970s. The leading PLO cadre from all the groups were elitists and—despite their radical rhetoric—traditionalists who held the common people in contempt. The majority of the masses were passive peasants or demoralized refugees whose inactivity was reinforced by the experience of defeat and of ridicule from other Arabs. Instead, their cultural tradition glorified a heroic minority whose model was the heritage of the tribal raid, Islamic holy war, and the single combat of the medieval wars against the crusaders. They would be willing to sacrifice themselves—the meaning of their name for the guerrillas, "Fedayeen"—to achieve liberation for the admiring audience.

The leaders of al-Fatah and the PLO had little taste for the delegation of authority required for mass organizing. They feared that local leaders might sell out to Israel, Jordan, or take over the movement themselves and ignore the PLO. Arafat's 1967 visit to the West Bank shortly after its capture by Israel seemed to persuade him of the impossibility of political organizing there. He found few activists—and they were pan-Arab rather than Palestinian nationalists. Israel's intelligence network was so good that it almost succeeded in catching him. This suggested that the struggle, at least in the beginning, would have to be organized outside the territories. A model for the PLO attitude toward those in the West Bank and Gaza was their disregard for Arabs who had remained in Israel after 1948. Although they were thought, rather inaccurately, to be enduring horrible suffering, their decision to stay made them politically suspect as collaborators; the presumed level of repression there made them unable to lead the struggle. When lines of communication between Israeli Arabs and West Bank residents were reopened in 1967, the former were seen to be largely coopted, economically prosperous, and politically quiescent.

Because the political mobilization of the masses against Israel was largely, if not completely, rejected, the PLO decided on armed struggle. Attacks were deliberately provocative to inspire a more intense Israeli reprisal, creating an escalating crisis that was intended to set the Arab states and their far more powerful armies into motion. Egyptian-sponsored terrorism against Israel in 1953-1956, the al-Fatah founders first military experience, did bring war, as did Palestinian terrorism in the 1965-1967 period. Although the 1967 defeat damaged the expectation that they would return to Palestine behind Egyptian and Syrian bayonets, PLO leaders thought they could afford to be impatient because they would not have to build their own force for a protracted war. The PLO leaders believed that the Arab states would do the main work of defeating Israel and that spectacular terrorist acts were a way to keep them engaged in the conflict, to make sure it stayed in the headlines and would neither be forgotten nor resolved.

If the violence created such bitterness between Israel and Arabs that they could not negotiate, that was all to the better. Because the PLO was not interested in diplomacy—an attitude that the smaller PLO and anti-Arafat groups continued into the 1980s—terrorism was an asset. Moreover, the more audacious and horrifying the act was to the outside, hostile world, the more it would draw the attention and admiration of Arab people and countries. The PLO was not trying to win U.S. or West European support—they were seen as irreversibly imperialist and pro-Israel—but rather Arab rulers' backing. Terrorism was meant to stir up Palestinians, to show them that Israel was being fought and defeated, to demonstrate revenge was being taken, and to highlight that Palestinian action outshown Arab leaders' speeches.

The compatible rationale for armed struggle was the PLO's attempt to copy the Marxist-Leninist revolutionaries of China, Cuba, and Vietnam in the doctrine of protracted "people's war" so popular among revolutionary theorists in the 1960s. This meant hit-and-run guerrilla tactics in rural areas, gradually building to a higher level of combat: bigger units, the seizure and holding of "liberated zones," and, finally, the march on cities and the enemy regime's collapse. PLO cadre avidly read Che Guevara and Mao Zedong and trained in Communist countries.[22]

The PLO found itself unable to follow this blueprint, however, its target was not a government, but a whole people. Marxist guerrilla struggles sought to overturn a regime, expel foreign influence, and win over the population. The PLO, on the other hand, sought to destroy—politically or physically—the existing community. It had no incentive to try to win over Israeli Jews.

In Mao Zedong's famous analogy, the people were supposed to be the fish among whom the guerrillas swam for concealment and help. But Israel was a sea full of sharks for any Palestinian guerrilla. Moreover, the saboteurs trying to penetrate the West Bank from Jordan sought to evade, rather than engage, a highly effective Israeli army trying to intercept and kill them. The PLO groups sought softer targets for their bombs and bullets.

During these years, dependence on terrorism also had a major effect on internal PLO politics. For example, those most successful in achieving terrorist acts accumulated prestige and power, which made them rise in al-Fatah. They were hardened in opposing moderation, loath to abandon an armed struggle that was their specialty, obsession, and source of authority. Because terrorism is best conducted by small, compartmented networks, reliance on this strategy increased the PLO's already excessive fragmentation. Groups inside and outside the PLO competed in staging spectacular actions to gain recruits and prestige. Smaller factions saw terrorism as their comparative advantage over al-Fatah: Because they could not compete in size, they had to compete in heroism, publicity, and military effectiveness.

Having conceded the propriety of terrorist armed struggle, Arafat and his colleagues could neither denounce it nor punish those seen as champions by the general Arab public. Once terrorism became so legitimate—the very currency of a proper struggle—its quantity and variety became a measure of the movement's success. Even a PLO Executive Committee member could admit, in a secret 1979 conversation, that PLO terrorism inside Israel was counterproductive, drawing attention away from West Bank political activity. But because Arafat's power rested on an activist reputation, he could not risk the criticism that he was doing nothing.[23]

This does not mean that the PLO was blind to the problems arising from its concentration on terrorism, but these actions were considered integral to the struggle. "No matter what the figures of probable and expected losses," said Arafat, "they will be nothing compared with the great goal."[24] If the PLO was unconcerned with Palestinian losses, it would hardly be deterred by those of its enemy or presumed allies.

Moreover, the PLO always thought what others considered terrorism to be justifiable armed struggle. After its first airplane hijacking in 1969, the PFLP explained: "We may have been obliged to violate international laws, under exceptional circumstances and against our will, but the Zionists have violated international law so often that it has become a matter of routine for them." Their alleged immoral behavior included, "Mass evictions of Arabs from their lands, collective murder and torture of school girls, who have been thrown into prison with Zionist prostitutes." Israeli airliners had also been used for military purposes. These views provided two standard justifications of terrorism by the PLO: exaggerated Zionist crimes and the concept that because any institution of Israel, including a kindergarten, was part of the existence and defense of an illegitimate state, they were all legitimate targets.[25]

Similarly, asked why his group planted a bomb in a Jerusalem food market, Habash said it was a reprisal for the shooting of a hijacker in Switzerland after he allegedly gave up, "And we will continue in this policy if the Israelis continue to drop napalm bombs on civilians and to torture our prisoners in the occupied territories."[26]

Airplane hijacking was a terrific way to grab international headlines. The July 1968 hijacking of a Rome-Tel Aviv El Al plane to Algiers was the first, and, throughout the next 14 years, there were 29 Palestinian hijackings. PLO groups also introduced attacks against aircraft and passengers on the ground—starting with a December 1968 PFLP attack on an El Al plane in Athens that killed one passenger—as well as blowing up planes in the air—beginning with a Popular Front for the Liberation of Palestine-General Command assault on Swissair's Zurich-Tel Aviv flight and an unsuccessful attempt against the Austrian airline in February 1970. The culmination was the September 1970 PFLP seizure of four planes simultaneously, which triggered the crisis in Jordan.

Terrorism was seen as retribution for longer-term suffering. Habash stressed to his Western hostages in Amman in September 1970,

> For 23 years we lived in misery and suffering in camps outside our country, driven like sheep, neglected, and waiting for our rights to be restored. And nothing happened. Then three years ago the course of events gave us the opportunity to take up arms for the cause of the liberation of our territory....You get up in the morning and have your coffee and milk. Your wives sit at the mirror for half an hour, or board planes to Geneva, while our wives are queueing for water in the camps. You live in dollar luxury, you travel and enjoy yourselves, so naturally you cannot feel as we do, just as we cannot think and feel as you do....We have no water to wash our faces, sometimes none to drink. If you visited our camps only once a week you would not be able to bear it, but we have to live in them all our lives.[27]

Consequently, he continued,

> We felt that we had the right to defend ourselves, bearing in mind our sufferings and our people. You in your world feel coolly towards us....Our law is our revolution. It is our duty to defend it because it is a righteous cause and because we shall be victorious. And it is our duty to liquidate the group that is conspiring against us....At least a thousand people have been killed or wounded in the fighting, as far as we can estimate. But we are very pleased that we have not been obliged to blow up the hotel over your heads. But if our camps had

been attacked again, we should not have hesitated to do so, we were deadly serious....I offer my personal apologies. Our men are excellent fighters, but I am not sure that they were very good at running a hotel.[28]

Thus, the comfortable West must suffer. But how did that help the Palestinians? The camps were terrible, but why did residents not accept resettlement? Were there real anti-Palestinian conspiracies or the mere responses of those seeking to defend themselves from the actions of the revolutionaries and terrorists? And, finally, what effect does it have on a revolution when it justifies everything? Thus, Hawatmeh could call a 1978 attack on a bus in which many civilians were killed, "a heroic operation stemming from the right of our people and our revolution to employ all forms of struggle."[29]

Although al-Fatah was very active in terrorist activities—this being one of the main reasons for its preeminence—the small groups were more dependent on using it to compete for a share of prestige and power. It was the only way factions with only a few hundred members could claim an equal role in Palestinian decision-making. The Palestine Liberation Front (PLF) was estimated to have 300 members split into three factions, each backed by a different Arab state. Yet one of those shards, headed by Abu al-'Abbas, generated world headlines, provided its leader with a seat on the PLO Executive Committee, and gave him the ability to disrupt Arafat's major diplomatic efforts in 1986 and 1990 through its spectacular terrorist assaults.[30]

Ironically, or not, the self-proclaimed Marxist DFLP and PFLP, which spoke of allying with progressive Jews and creating a secular democratic state, were most bloodthirsty. For them, ideology provided a license to kill. Their goal of world revolution broadened their range of targets, and acceptance of Syrian sponsorship made them surrogates for specific terror operations or campaigns. Any centralization, moderation, or compromise required by diplomacy made them eager to use terror to block an alleged impending compromise with conservative Arabs or the United States. And finally, they needed to escalate violence to stake their claim against al-Fatah or at least remind the world, Arabs, and Palestinians that they still existed.

Moreover, by so frightening and hardening Israelis, the strategy of terrorism blocked any political consensus or majority in Israel for negotiating with the PLO or agreeing to a West Bank/Gaza Palestinian state. Not only were Arafat's hands stained with blood, it was argued, but there was no reason to believe that he, even in the pursuit of total victory, would be able or willing to stop further terrorism even after a state was established.

Terrorism, however, proved ineffective as a means of conquering Israel, as well as diplomatically destructive. To a point, terrorism helped publicize the PLO's cause and won some Western concessions, especially in Europe. Ultimately, the terrorist strategy damaged the group's standing in the United States and Western Europe, while making Israel adamant in refusing to negotiate with the PLO, skeptical of Arab intentions, and more unwilling to yield territory that might be used as a base by terrorists. In an almost unique critique of the terrorist strategy, a Palestinian intellectual wrote, "Too many of us feel that we have gained representation and media visibility at an exorbitant cost. We became known as hijackers and terrorists."[31]

Terrorism was thus a mixed blessing for the PLO's political goals. It helped Arafat maintain a posture of leadership, activism, and success, while concurrently contributing to his inability to negotiate with the United States or Israel for many years. On May 20, 1990, Abu al-'Abbas's forces launched a major sea attack against Israel. The terrorists were killed or captured by Israeli forces. Arafat neither denounced the raid nor punished Abu al-'Abbas. In response, the United States suspended the U.S.-PLO dialogue. It was yet one more example of the high cost of terrorism for the PLO and the Palestinian people.

Notes

1. Merari book, p. 5; *Ma'ariv*, October 18, 1985 from Ministry of Foreign Affairs, *White Book*.

2. *Third World Quarterly* 8 no. 2, (April 1986); "Yassir Arafat," As Khalid al-Hasan explained, "For us, military action is something that this is no way the subject of any discussion except from the premise that it will be intensified both in scope and nature." *Al-Riyad*, December 5, 1978. Translation in JPRS No. 72836, February 16, 1979. Syria offered a new definition of terrorism to the United Nations in 1987. Violence by "national liberation movements" was good; violence—even in self-defense—by "racist" and "colonial" states was terrorism. Presumably, Damascus did not intend this definition to apply to the Islamic fundamentalists in Hama or Iraqi- directed

"freedom fighters" in London.

3. *Filastin al-Thawra*, June 1968, Harkabi, p. 9.

4. Ibrahim Sous, *Nouvelle Observateur*, August 14, 1981.

5. Arafat called Algeria a "very useful experience from which we have learned a great deal." Interview, *International Documents on Palestine* (hereafter referred to as IDOP) 1969, pp. 691-692.

6. "Yassir Arafat," *Third World Quarterly 8*, no. 2 (April 1986); Harkabi, op. cit., p. 12: *al-Anwar* symposium of 3/8/70; Arafat interview of May 1969 in *IDOP* 1969, pp 691-692.

7. *IDOP*, 1969, p. 400.

8. Interview with Arafat, *Al-Usbu' al-'Arabi*, January 22, 1968 in IDOP, 1968, p. 300.

9. *Filastin al-Thawra*, January 1970, p. 8.

10. Israeli, op. cit., p. 31.

11. Interview in *Al-Ahram*, February 21, 1985. Translation in *Journal of Palestine Studies* 14, no. 3 (Spring 1985): 151-153.

12. Abu Iyad interview, June 1969, in *IDOP* 1969, p. 732.

13. Habash, mid-May 1970, *IDOP* 1970, p. 805.

14. Husayn al-Umari (Abu Ibrahim) split from the PFLP in 1979 to form the May 15 organization. In 1982, this group bombed a U.S. airliner en route to Hawaii, killing 1 and injuring 14 passengers. In December 1983, it tried to blow up three airliners, and, in January 1984, it tried and failed to bomb an El Al plane. Ahmad Jibril, leader of the PFLP-GC, was born around 1935 in Ramla, Palestine. His family left in 1948 to Qunaytra, Syria, and in 1954, he joined the Syrian army. He became an engineer captain, but in 1958 was dismissed by a conservative government for radical activities. He then joined forces with Syrian radicals who seized power in 1963 and was ever-after aligned with Syria. U.S. Department of State, *PFLP-GC*, November 14, 1988 Fact Sheet. On Habash, see statement of mid-May 1970, in *IDOP* 1970, p. 804.

15. George Habash, July 25, 1970, *IDOP* 1970, pp. 878-882. At any rate, Habash was skeptical about the value of public opinion: "Our idea of the battle of liberation is that it will not be won through the sympathy of world public opinion; it will be won through our own masses, their awareness of their cause, their organization, their mobilization, their bearing arms, their reliance on themselves, their fighting day after day, inflicting slight damage on the enemy here and there, and their preparedness to offer millions of victims until victory is won."

16. Al-Azm, "The Palestinian Resistance Movement Reconsidered," 130.

17. Paul Jureidini and William Hazen, *The Palestinian Movement in Politics* (Lexington, Mass., 1976), 16.

18. *Washington Post*, October 15, 1987.

19. *The Economist*, October 3, 1970.

20. Moshe Maoz, "The Palestinian Guerrilla Organizations and the Soviet Union," in Moshe Maos, *Palestinian Arab Politics* (Jerusalem, 1975), 98.

21. "The PLO Papers," *The Economist*, July 10, 1982, p. 48.

22. For one of many examples of this thinking, see Gerard Chaliand, *The Palestinian Resistance*.

23. David Hirst, "The Other Hostage in Beirut," *Guardian*, June 30, 1985, p. 7; Nashashibi in May 3, 1979, U.S. State Department dispatch by Newton, May 3, 1979, *Den of Spies*, Vol. 42, pp. 7-9.

24. Arafat interview, August 1968, *IDOP* 1968, p. 413.

25. PFLP statement, February 1, 1969, *IDOP* 1969, pp. 597-598.

26. Habash interview, March 4, 1969, *IDOP* 1969, pp. 630-631.

27. *Arab World*, *IDOP* 1970, pp. 836-839, Speech by Habash to Foreign Hostages Held in the Intercontinental Hotel in Amman, June 12, 1970.

28. Ibid.

29. Hawatmeh, April 22, 1978, *Journal of Palestine Studies* 12, no. 4 (Summer 1978): 192.

30. The three factions were those of Tal'at Yaqub in Syria, Abu al-'Abbas in Iraq, and Abd al-Fatah Ghanem in Libya. The PLF emerged from the PFLP-GC after Jibril supported Syria's 1976 attacks on the PLO in Lebanon. It entered the PNC in 1981 and split over the attitude of the rebels against al-Fatah in 1983 and 1984, with Abu al-'Abbas backing Arafat.

31. Moughrabi, p. 214.

Index